Collective Identity, Oppression, and the Right to Self-Ascription

Collective Identity, Oppression, and the Right to Self-Ascription

Andrew J. Pierce

LEXINGTON BOOKS
Lanham • Boulder • New York • Toronto • Plymouth, UK

Published by Lexington Books
A wholly owned subsidiary of The Rowman & Littlefield Publishing Group, Inc.
4501 Forbes Boulevard, Suite 200, Lanham, Maryland 20706
www.rowman.com

10 Thornbury Road, Plymouth PL6 7PP, United Kingdom

Copyright © 2012 by Lexington Books

All rights reserved. No part of this book may be reproduced in any form or by any electronic or mechanical means, including information storage and retrieval systems, without written permission from the publisher, except by a reviewer who may quote passages in a review.

British Library Cataloguing in Publication Information Available

Library of Congress Cataloging-in-Publication Data

Pierce, Andrew J., 1981-
Collective identity, oppression, and the right to self-ascription / Andrew J. Pierce.
p. cm.
Includes bibliographical references and index.
ISBN 978-0-7391-7190-5 (alk. paper) -- ISBN 978-0-7391-7191-2 (electronic)
1. Group identity. 2. Social groups. 3. Ethnicity. I. Title.
HM753.P528 2012
305.8--dc23
2012010656

∞™ The paper used in this publication meets the minimum requirements of American National Standard for Information Sciences Permanence of Paper for Printed Library Materials, ANSI/NISO Z39.48-1992.

Printed in the United States of America

Table of Contents

Acknowledgments — vii

Introduction — 1

1. Minority Cultures and Oppressed Groups: Competing Explanatory Frameworks — 11
2. Collective Identity, Group Rights, and the Liberal Tradition of Law — 39
3. Identity Politics within the Limits of Deliberative Democracy — 69
4. The Future of Racial Identity: A Test Case — 99

Bibliography — 127

Index — 131

Acknowledgments

This book would not have been possible without the support of many individuals and institutions. Conversations and courses with Stephen Esquith, Marilyn Frye, Bill Lawson, Richard Peterson, and Lisa Schwartzman helped me to begin thinking about questions of collective identity and how they related to issues of oppression, cultural membership and liberal political philosophy. Jennifer Parks and Tom Wren provided helpful feedback in the early stages of the project, as did Jackie Scott and David Schweickart, whose ongoing, insightful guidance undoubtedly prevented many wrong turns and potential mistakes. I would also like to thank Charles Mills for his helpful comments and guidance at various stages of the process, and for taking the time to work with and mentor a young philosopher outside of the auspices of official faculty responsibilities. Most importantly, I would like to thank David Ingram, for ongoing guidance and encouragement at every stage of the process, and for being a wonderful mentor in general. If this book makes a valuable contribution, it is surely because of his tutelage. Additionally, I would like to thank the Arthur J. Schmitt Foundation for its generous support, which allowed me to give the book my undivided attention, and to finish it in a timely manner. Finally, I would like to thank my friends and family, whose love and support have been critical not just to this project, but to all of my endeavors academic and otherwise. You know who you are.

Introduction

Traditional liberal political theory is characterized in large part by its focus on individuals and individual rights. That is, it begins with the presumption that the collective political life of citizens is preceded (if not historically, at least conceptually) by a state of nature in which each individual is sovereign. This complete and brutal freedom necessitates a social contract that places limits on individuals for the sake of law and order, but ultimately, the goal of such a contract is to preserve as much of the original freedom of the individual as possible. This standard trope is familiar to any student of political philosophy, as are the many criticisms that have been leveled against it. These criticisms vary widely, but many revolve around the claim that individuals did or could preexist the social relationships that make us who we are, objecting that individuals are constituted by these very relationships, as their product, in some sense, and not their precondition. More recent liberal theory has tried to speak to such criticisms by acknowledging the importance of group memberships and social relationships to individual identity and even individual citizenship. Thus theorists like Will Kymlicka, Charles Taylor, Michael Sandel, Michael Walzer, and others aim to preserve liberal principles of freedom and equality while acknowledging that human beings are social creatures whose individuality in many ways depends upon certain group memberships and affinities.

On a related, but nonetheless distinct front, political movements organized around *identity*—race, gender, ethnicity, sexual orientation, and so on—have taken a central place in the contemporary political landscape. And while these various movements, grouped together under the moniker of 'identity politics,' differ significantly, some vehemently opposing liberalism and others framing their politics squarely within the liberal tradition, mainstream liberalism has almost unequivocally objected to identity politics on the grounds that it allows for grave injustices to individuals, undermines the pursuit of universal social justice, and with its "balkanizing" effects, generally destabilizes the very foundations of civil society.

In this book, I argue that such criticisms are unwarranted, though their purveyors are right at least in noticing that identity politics of a certain sort (namely, the politics of *oppressed* groups) does represent a significantly different approach to group membership and group rights than the dominant liberal approach, which I call "multicultural liberalism." The first chapter, then, outlines this dominant approach as well as its shortcomings, including, perhaps most importantly, that it fails to adequately address or even acknowledge a whole set of group-based injustices—those involving oppression. This is not surprising, I suggest, since oppression is premised upon group membership, while multicultural liberalism still sees group rights as ultimately derivative of the rights of individuals. That is, the paradigm of group membership for liberalism is the voluntary association, and cultural groups are understood primarily as providing contexts for individual choice, including even the choice to participate in the culture itself. Whether or not this is an accurate account of cultural groups (and there are good reasons to think it is not) it certainly does not capture the essence of oppressed groups, membership in which is decidedly *not* a matter of individual choice, but is instead ascribed by forces outside of the individual's control.

Will Kymlicka is the primary target of my critique here, insofar as his version of multicultural liberalism is the most explicit about accounting for communitarian and multicultural critiques *within* a fairly traditionally liberal framework (based, that is, on the idea of *individual* freedom). Kymlicka argues, for example, that cultural membership must be considered one of the basic goods that individuals require in order to pursue whatever other ends they might aspire to.[1] Therefore any schema of distributive justice must assure and protect cultural membership just as it assures and protects other basic goods, such as political representation, equality of opportunity, income and wealth, and so on. For the majority, such access to cultural membership is mostly unproblematic. For those "minority cultures," however, whose cultural identity may come to be threatened in various ways, special rights and protections may be justified. Kymlicka thus argues that certain group rights—rights to sovereignty, for example—can be justified on liberal grounds for certain kinds of cultural minorities.

The main problem with such an approach is that it fails to account for some of the most normatively pressing group-based injustices, those experienced by oppressed groups. And insofar, I argue, as oppression is premised upon group membership, an account of group rights based upon the (individual) freedom-securing function of culture will do little to clarify or mitigate these sorts of injustices. That is, unlike cultural groups, which can be understood as depending on the conscious, collective intentionality of their individual members, as well as providing a precondition for their individual freedoms, oppressed groups are non-intentional, or "ascriptive"—formed and maintained by external forces—and limiting, rather than enabling of the freedom of their members. This is not only, or even primarily, a descriptive difference in the kinds of groups that exist, but a theoretical difference in the way one understands group membership. That is, I suggest that not only are the accounts of Kymlicka and other multicultural liberals too narrow to account for many if not most social groups, but worse, that their "cultural" approach misses important dimensions even of the specific types of groups it aims to investigate. It misses, for example, the important differences between those immigrant groups that integrate more or less successfully into the dominant political, legal, and social structures, and those that, for a variety of reasons including especially issues of racism and economic exploitation, become ghettoized and remain unassimilated. It also misses important differences between those groups that have become national minorities through confederation or other more or less peaceful means, and those that have been minoritized through processes of conquest, colonization, and other forms of violence. It seems reasonable to think that such differences might matter for determining what types of group rights can legitimately be claimed by the groups in question.

Accordingly, then, I suggest that an analysis of group rights should begin from considerations of oppression rather than considerations of culture, and should further recognize that, since oppression is a kind of *group* harm, irreducible to the individual harms experienced by group members, group rights aimed at remediating such harms are also irreducible to the individual rights of group members. In other words, I argue that certain group rights must be understood as rights possessed by groups qua group-hood, and not rights possessed by groups qua individual group members. In particular, I argue that groups possess a right to *self-ascription*, understood as a right to determine the meaning and extent of group membership. Oppression is the paradigmatic violation of this right.

The first chapter, then, draws from important work on oppression done by Marilyn Frye, Ann Cudd, Sally Haslanger, and others. It draws also from the work of Charles Mills, which I argue can be thought of in terms of oppression, as well as the "realist" social ontology of Paul Sheehy, which provides a basis for thinking about groups as irreducible social entities.

The second chapter further explains and supports the idea of a right to self-ascription, drawing from Jürgen Habermas's discursive justification of rights and the communicative intersubjectivity upon which it is ultimately based. Habermas's rich body of work provides a unique model of how norms implicit in communication bind us together in discourse. That is, it shows how effective communication presupposes mutual agreement on norms of truth, rightness, and sincerity. The grounding of communication in mutually recognized norms (undertaken primarily in *The Theory of Communicative Action*) makes *intersubjectivity* the foundation upon which Habermas develops his moral, political, and legal theory. This foundational intersubjectivity provides the philosophical basis for the right to self-ascription.

Given this foundational intersubjectivity, it is somewhat surprising that in the places where Habermas explicitly discusses group rights and the "claims of cultures," he defends a conception of law that is "individualistic in form."[2] I begin the second chapter by looking at this claim and showing that, while Habermas recognizes that the idea of positive law entails that individuals are the bearers of rights, the democratic justification of law points to a prior communicative intersubjectivity. That is, insofar as individual rights are themselves only justified discursively, the kind of intersubjectivity that makes discursive justification possible must be seen as the precondition for individual rights. Further, I argue, this intersubjectivity is not just the abstract intersubjectivity of communicative competence, but the concrete intersubjectivity of collective identity.

The extent to which a shared collective identity of some kind is a necessary condition for citizenship or political participation is another central theme of communitarianism and multicultural liberalism. And though Habermas rejects the communitarian claim that citizenship is or should be based on a strong "ethical-cultural" identity, he nonetheless admits that a weaker, "ethical-political" identity is necessary to provide the kind of solidarity constitutive of any effective political community. Moreover, Habermas sees particular identity groups as playing an important role in expanding the scope of supposedly universal rights as, for example, the civil rights movement and the "feminist politics of equality" did. In many ways, then, I argue, collective identity and real-world collectivities are central to and even foundational for Habermas's discourse theory of democracy and individual rights.

Similar claims have been pressed by students and scholars of Habermas, especially feminist philosophers and critical theorists like Seyla Benhabib, Nancy Fraser, Simone Chambers, Drucilla Cornell, and others. Fraser argues, for example, that healthy democratic deliberation is exemplified by a plurality of counterpublics—identity groups engaged in discourses of self-clarification and interpretation of their collective identities—rather than a single, overarching public sphere. My discussion of Habermas, as well as the explication of the right to self-ascription, builds upon some of these critics. Still, none to my knowledge develops a systematic approach to political discourses on identity in order to provide a discursive normative foundation for identity politics in general.

Habermas's reflections on democracy, rights, and intersubjectivity help to clarify the meaning of a right to self-ascription. It becomes clear, in particular, that the right to self-ascription is not a legal right in the specific sense. Rather, it must be understood as a moral right that undergirds and makes possible legal rights, insofar as those rights depend upon intersubjective processes of discursive justification. A right to self-ascription, then, is based upon respect for the formative character of intersubjectivity (formative in the sense that it gives rise to the content of individual rights, through discourse, but also in the sense that it is a precondition for individuation in general) and the necessity of self-ascribed identity groups for healthy democratic functioning.

Yet, as helpful as Habermas is, the strict proceduralism of his later work does not illuminate the ways in which intersubjectivity could give rise to something like a right to self-ascription. This is because, insofar as a right to self-ascription is, I argue, a precondition for discursive justification, it cannot itself be justified by discursive procedures alone. Rather, I suggest that the right to self-ascription must be justified by *substantive* argumentation. In making a substantive case for such a right, then, I draw from the recognition-based theory of another student of Habermas, Axel Honneth, as well as the capability theory of Martha Nussbaum and Amartya Sen. I conclude that the right to self-ascription must be seen as having an intrinsic value, in addition to its instrumental value in making possible individual rights of the type discussed above, and that it can be understood as providing a model of *intersubjective* human flourishing: an ideal of associational life that is not exhausted in or reducible to the ideal of the flourishing individual.

The third chapter examines the ways in which such a right provides a foundation for contemporary identity politics. In particular, it circumscribes the *limits* of the right to self-ascription, based on a set of principles derived from Habermas's "discourse ethic." In this way, a major criticism of identity politics—that it cannot make normative distinctions among the demands of different identity groups—is circumvented. In short, I argue that taking identity politics seriously does not require claiming that any and all identity groups deserve equal (or any) recognition. Here procedural criteria allow one to *avoid* making substantive judgments about the *content* of particular identity constructions, while nonetheless explaining why certain identity groups (for example, hate groups and other "illiberal" groups) need not be granted rights and accommodations that other groups deserve and require.

In making this argument, I distinguish between two kinds of identity politics. "Retributive" identity politics asserts as a matter of strategy that the best and most consistent advocate for ending the oppression of a particular identity group is that group itself. It thus asserts that women must join together to fight patriarchy, gays must join together to fight heterosexism, African Americans must join together to fight antiblack racism, and so on. This does not imply, I claim, that such groups must be concerned *only* with their own oppression, nor that no one but a particular group should be concerned with that group's oppression. Still, the rules of discourse outlined by the discourse ethic are not particularly useful for understanding identity politics of this sort, in part because the fight against oppression makes necessary certain kinds of strategic exclusions, insincere posturing, and other tactics that might not be justified under ideally just circumstances. Retributive identity politics basically concerns the best means for eliminating oppression and as such falls squarely within the scope of so-called "nonideal" theory.

"Discursive-democratic" identity politics, however, is distinct from identity politics aimed at eliminating oppression. The distinction derives from the thought that collective identities, being crucially important to the constitution of personal identities and political interests, will not cease to be politically salient even under ideal conditions. Discursive-democratic identity politics thus aims to specify an appropriate relation between identity groups and the society/state at large. Here, I suggest, is where an adaptation of the discourse ethic is illuminating. I argue that the kinds of group identity that are justifiable within the context of a democratic social order are those that approximate the rules of discourse internally. They must be open and inclusive (to a certain degree), provide equal opportunity for the growth and development of their members, and be adopted sincerely and without coercion. The application of these conditions or "rules" to the process of collective identity formation requires taking certain liberties with the discourse ethic as Habermas explicitly develops it, but I argue that such liberties are justified and perhaps even implied in a certain way by Habermas's own analyses.

What such an application provides is a picture of the "social construction of identity" that is both descriptive and normative. It is descriptive in the sense that it aims to describe what identity construction would look like under ideal (non-oppressive) conditions, and it is normative in the sense that it aims to identify principles according to which claims for recognition can be judged. In this way it is analogous to the discourse ethic proper, which holds that the agreements of interlocutors engaged in discourse are normatively binding in part because such norms are involved in the way persons *actually do* communicate with one another. Still, I argue that the normativity of discursive principles of collective identity formation is not best understood in terms of coercive rules and regulations, but rather in terms of "normal" development and functioning. That is, identities that require recognition and accommodation are those that provide for their members the benefits typical of collective identity. The burden of the argument is thus to show that those groups that fail to meet the requirements of discourse also fail, as a result, to provide such benefits.

I end the chapter by considering how the right to self-ascription and the kind of identity politics that is derived from it relate to traditional concerns for material wealth and distributive justice. I argue that attempts to correlate identity politics with recognition and reserve concerns for distribution for some other kind of politics are mistaken. Identity politics is perfectly capable of accounting for concerns of distribution, and in fact most identity-based movements have given a central place to such concerns in their explicit political programs. Further, I show that concerns of material wealth—unemployment, wage discrepancies, and so on—are a major reason why certain illiberal groups continue to exist despite the lack of communicative resources they provide for their members. In making this argument, I look to the interesting and fruitful debate between Fraser and Honneth presented in their dialogue on redistribution and recognition.[3] I draw also from key contributions to the philosophy and politics of identity from theorists like Linda Alcoff, Amy Gutmann, and others.

In the fourth and final chapter, I show how this theory of discursive identity formation can be applied fruitfully to current debates about race and racial identity. I take it that biological theories of race, which understand race as a biological natural kind, have been thoroughly debunked. Most race theorists agree that race is a social construction, drawing more or less arbitrarily upon certain physical and/or phenomenal features of persons. But the political implications of this basic agreement are far from clear. Some have taken it to mean that we ought to stop talking about "races" as though they were real and work to develop other kinds of identifications to replace so-called "racial" identities. Others have suggested that, though race may not be ontologically "real," political structures that take races as basic make race an unavoidable social reality. And others still have argued that racial identity can be reinterpreted in such a way as to shed its deterministic connotations but retain important features that have come to flourish under the oppressive force of, say, black identity. In short, the fact that race is "socially constructed," as important an insight as it is, tells us relatively little about what role, if any, race ought to play in a more just social order and in the construction of legitimate group identities.

Current debates about racial identity provide a useful point of application since one of their central questions is whether a collective identity that has been constructed largely as a means of oppression can be reconstructed in a normatively justifiable way, or whether it must be abandoned altogether. It considers, in other words, the possibility of transforming an oppressive, ascriptive identity into a positive, self-ascribed identity, precisely the process that I outline in general philosophical terms. Using the discursive-democratic model of identity construction as a guide, then, my aim is to determine whether racial identity would be justifiable under ideal, non-oppressive conditions. I conclude that discursively justifiable racial identities are conceivable, separable from their origins in ascriptive, oppressive practices, though I stop short of the claim that racial identities are a *necessary* or inevitable feature of social organization.

I begin, then, by presenting a brief genealogy of the idea of race, then engage in the debates, undertaken by Anthony Appiah, Naomi Zack, Lucius Outlaw, and others, as to whether that history demands a wholesale rejection of racial concepts or whether some notion of race remains necessary or desirable. I argue, against Appiah and other "racial eliminativists," that race can be uncoupled from racial oppression, such that some conception of race might be discursively justifiable. I then discuss two kinds or conceptions of racial identity, mestizo racial identity and white racial identity. I argue that something like mestizo racial identity could be discursively justified, while white racial identity, insofar as it is inextricable linked to white supremacy, cannot. Having provided examples of both acceptable and unacceptable conceptions of racial identity, I end by returning to the question of culture and examining specifically the attempts to understand African American racial identity in cultural terms. I argue there, against certain varieties of "cultural nationalism," that it is unwise to think of African Americans as a culture in the thick sense of the term that multicultural liberals employ.

Though this book draws heavily from what I take to be an original and useful interpretation of Habermas (with, of course, important precedents that I have pointed to above), it is ultimately topical. I mean to present a normative account of group formation and group identity that resolves some of the enduring problems in liberal multicultural theory, as well as provides a firmer foundation for identity politics, which has too often been attacked for being a flimsy sort of anything-goes relativism, or for reducing politics to issues of personal identity. I use racial identity as a test case for the discursive account of identity because it is, as Kymlicka points out, a difficult case, and one that has not received the same attention as other kinds of (cultural, ethnic, and gender) identity. If a discursive account of identity is useful, it ought to be able to provide an answer to the question of whether racial identities are legitimate in an ideal democratic polity. That is, if race is "socially constructed," as we often hear, a discursive norm of identity formation ought to suggest parameters for its legitimate reconstruction.

Habermas's discourse ethical mode of justification has stimulated much discussion in recent political and moral philosophy, but much of this discussion understands the theory in relative isolation from its roots in the theory of communicative action, choosing instead to see it as a more or less freestanding theory similar in some respects to Rawls's original position. Habermas himself sometimes seems to lend credence to such an interpretation, despite his relatively minor criticisms of the Rawlsian project. Yet the application of the discursive mode of justification in real-world scenarios raises a distinct set of issues regarding group identity and inclusion. If, as Habermas admits, the justification of moral norms relies upon real-world communities, then "solidarity is simply the reverse side of justice."[4] And if, as one would expect, solidarity has its limits (that it is, at least in some respects, a function of group membership), then the question of groups becomes central to the Habermasian project. That is, groups would appear, then, to be the fundamental units of Habermas's liberal democratic theory and not a special problem for liberalism, as they often appear for theorists like Kymlicka. This question of priority is even more pressing given that Habermas's recent engagement with multicultural and cosmopolitan theory has brought problems of ethnic and national identity to the forefront of his thinking.

Moreover, the relatively recent growth of race theory, which promises to make substantial contributions to philosophical knowledge, and perhaps even to the vital political task of reorganizing racial relations in the United States and other racially divided nations, has occurred largely in isolation from that Habermasian strand of critical theory that becomes ever more abstract as it considers the rational and linguistic preconditions for consensus, but not the social and political preconditions for actual public discourses. For identifying the latter, conversations across race theory and critical theory would prove, I think, quite fruitful. In the most general terms, then, this is what the following pages aim to do.

NOTES

1. Will Kymlicka, *Multicultural Citizenship: A Liberal Theory of Minority Rights* (Oxford: Oxford University Press, 1995).

2. See especially Habermas's essay on "Struggles for Recognition in the Democratic State" in Charles Taylor's *Multiculturalism: Examining the Politics of Recognition.* edited by Amy Gutmann. (Princeton: Princeton University Press, 1994); as well as "Equal Treatment of Cultures and the Limits of Postmodern Liberalism," *The Journal of Political Philosophy* 13, no. 1 (2005): 1-28.

3. Nancy Fraser and Axel Honneth, *Redistribution or Recognition: A Political-Philosophical Exchange* (London: Verso, 2003).

4. Jürgen Habermas, *The Inclusion of the Other: Studies in Political Theory*, trans. William Rehg (Cambridge: MIT Press, 1999): 14.

Chapter One

Minority Cultures and Oppressed Groups

Competing Explanatory Frameworks

In recent years, communitarians and other theorists have developed a critique of traditional liberalism that focuses on its inadequate understanding of cultural membership and other group affinities, often tracing this deficiency to liberalism's tendency to focus methodologically on individuals rather than groups.[1] More recent liberalism has tried to speak to this deficiency by giving liberal justifications for the protection of minority cultures. One might see such a *multicultural* liberalism as promising for addressing the concerns of other sorts of group harms, harms like racism, sexism, class exploitation, and so on. In fact, the tendency to focus on minority cultures of a specific type is often presented as an intentional limitation of scope, one which could be developed and expanded to justify retributive measures for other sorts of groups (say, racial minorities, women, or the poor).[2] However, I will argue that the strategies for dealing with the concerns of such groups, namely *oppressed* groups, are fundamentally different and even *incommensurable* with the types of liberal justifications given for the protection of minority cultures, for at least two reasons: (1) Multicultural liberalism presumes that cultures are complete and self-sufficient, and come into conflict only accidentally, while theories of oppression understand conflict as constitutive of group formation; and (2) despite concerns for certain types of groups and a willingness to grant certain types of "group rights," the methodology of multicultural liberalism is still ultimately individualist, while theories of oppression take groups as their fundamental conceptual units.

MINORITY CULTURES

The term "culture" is used in a variety of ways and with a certain ambiguity. One hears reference to Western culture, but also American culture and African American culture. It is not uncommon also to speak of workplace culture, capitalist culture, and so on. Culture thus sometimes seems to refer to the beliefs, customs, practices, and experiences held by a particular group of people, and sometimes it seems to refer to the group itself. The difference is not inconsequential. If culture refers in the first place to customs and practices, then one might think that persons enjoy a certain agency in relation to the sorts of practices they adopt; that customs and practices, in other words, are among the social goods that individuals choose to pursue. But if cultures refer in the first place to the groups themselves, then culture seems more like an identity than a social good, and one might think that it is more a constitutive condition of agency than an object of choice. Ranjoo Seodu Herr points to something like this distinction by differentiating between liberal autonomy and generic valuational agency.[3] Her point is that culture not only provides a range of meaningful choices required for autonomy, but that it also *limits* the range of choices available to individuals. This is an important insight, since multicultural theorists tend to equivocate between the two notions of culture, as I will show. But Herr does not challenge, nor see the need to challenge the liberal presumption that individuals are primary, and so she cannot explain why the dominant approach to protecting minority cultures fails when generalized to other kinds of groups. I will begin, then, by looking at multicultural liberalism with this question in mind.

Will Kymlicka's seminal work *Multicultural Citizenship* asserts a theory of group rights situated within the liberal tradition and based upon the conceptual categories of national minorities and ethnic groups. National minorities are "previously self-governing" groups, groups that, whether by conquest, colonization, or confederation, have fallen under the rule of a majority government that is not their own.[4] Native Americans and francophone Canadians, for example, are included in the category of national minorities. Ethnic groups, on the other hand, are groups that have voluntarily immigrated to another nation, and seek, more or less, to assimilate to its political structure as citizens. Kymlicka then goes on to try to specify what kinds of rights and protections each type of group can claim within a liberal framework of justification. The rights that ethnic groups can claim are limited, since those who voluntarily immigrate to a nation can reasonably be expected to integrate to the dominant culture, within certain limits. If such groups are to claim any sort of special rights or protections, then they must be remedial, aimed at eventual integration. But national minorities are a different case.

Kymlicka argues that for national minorities, special rights and protections are justified, up to and including rights to political autonomy and exemption from the laws of the dominant culture.

His analysis is not meant to be exhaustive. He admits that the status of African Americans, for example, is "very unusual" and fits neither model. He explains:

> [African Americans] do not fit the voluntary immigrants pattern, not only because they were brought to America involuntarily as slaves, but also because they were prevented (rather than encouraged) from integrating into the institutions of the majority culture . . . Nor do they fit the national minority pattern, since they do not have a homeland in America or a common historical language.[5]

He also recognizes that the "new social movements" representing those who "have been marginalized within their own national society or ethnic group" (he mentions gays, women, the poor, and the disabled) raise their own distinctive issues.[6] Iris Marion Young, in her critique of Kymlicka's framework of national and ethnic groups, expands the list of those groups that appear anomalous within this framework.[7] She points out that refugees, guest workers, former colonial subjects, and others do not fit neatly into the dichotomy of national and ethnic groups either. As it turns out then, Kymlicka's classificatory scheme fails to account for quite a large portion of those groups that populate contemporary multicultural societies. This is, in the first place, because Kymlicka employs a "thick" conception of culture.

This thick conception specifies the term "culture" by reference to what he calls "societal culture." A societal culture is "a culture which provides its members with meaningful ways of life across the full range of human activities, including social, educational, religious, recreational, and economic life."[8] Such a culture must be embodied in institutions, including governments, schools, economies, and so forth. A societal culture is thus an *institutionally embodied* culture that is more or less complete (providing meaning "across the full range of human activities"). The result of this thick conception of culture is that it drastically narrows the set of groups that count as cultures. Since immigrants, for example, generally do not have separate institutions within the countries to which they immigrate, only national minorities really count as minority cultures in the strict sense.[9] And though Kymlicka denies that all Americans share a common culture, he does go so far as to claim that there is a "dominant culture that incorporates most Americans, and those who fall outside it belong to a relatively small number of minority cultures."[10] Ultimately, then, Kymlicka sees a given territorial state containing within it a dominant culture and a few minority cultures.

If one accepts Kymlicka's thick conception of societal culture, it makes a certain amount of sense that only a few groups within any given state count as cultures, since there are only so many institutional structures that can fit, so to speak, within a given society. If all cultures in a looser sense were deemed societal cultures in Kymlicka's sense, one would be claiming that they all have (or at least have a right to) separate and complete institutional structures. If one thinks about the way "culture" is often used (Italian American culture, gay and lesbian culture, popular culture), one can immediately see that this claim would be inadequate both as a description of social reality and as a norm. It would be nearly impossible, and probably undesirable, for each of these groups to retain their own governments, economies, and so on. As Kymlicka rightly points out, this underestimates the "impressive integrative power" of the United States and perhaps "American culture" generally. Yet Kymlicka overestimates its power, overlooking serious integration problems and important differences within the "dominant culture." His social ontology thus runs the risk of concealing integration problems in groups that do not fall under his very stringent category of minority cultures. Further, understanding culture in this way leads Kymlicka to overlook important differences among those who supposedly share the same "cultural" institutions. Before developing this argument, however, let me consider another important representative of multicultural liberalism.

The employment of a thick conception of culture, and the problems that it raises, is not unique to Kymlicka. In fact, it is characteristic of many multicultural liberals, if not multicultural liberalism generally. Charles Taylor, for example, makes use of a similarly broad conception of culture, which gives rise to similar criticisms. Though Taylor does not define culture as explicitly as Kymlicka does (and, surprisingly, not at all in his essay *Multiculturalism*) his conception of culture can be clarified by his more recent work.

In *Multiculturalism*, Taylor attempts to disclose the historical-theoretical underpinnings of contemporary debates about political representation of cultural minorities, as well as controversies over multicultural curriculum.[11] He explicates these issues in terms of two political principles: The "politics of equal dignity" requires the assumption that individuals (and later in the book, "cultures") are of equal value. No one is assumed to be of greater value than another simply by reason of birth, lineage, social position, and so forth. The "politics of difference," on the other hand, requires recognition of one's individual identity, that which makes that person not only unique but authentic. This latter principle is derived from the former, in that part of what it means to treat individuals equally is recognizing the unique value of their particular identity. These two principles together make up the "politics of recognition." Problems arise, however, in negotiating the precarious balance between these two principles; that is, in trying to specify what it means to treat people *equally differently* in particular cases. Taylor points out two kinds of examples. On the one hand, political problems (in a narrow sense) arise when representing a particular cultural group equally (francophone Canadians, for example) requires granting special rights or protections. On the other hand, problems in the sphere of secondary and higher education arise when the assumption of the equal worth of a particular culture can only genuinely be made by careful study of that particular culture's literary and artistic contributions; by enacting a "fusion of horizons" between it and one's own culturally-bound worldview.[12]

The latter problem is largely pedagogical and beyond the scope of my analysis. The political problem is of more immediate concern, as the reader will see. But I mention these problems in the first place only in order to try to identify the conception of culture that binds them together. In both cases, we are asked to evaluate a demand for recognition: political representation in the first case; and representation in the literary canon in the second. Both have to do, in Taylor's words, "with the imposition of some cultures on others, and with the assumed superiority that powers this imposition."[13] So Taylor, like Kymlicka, appears to oppose "dominant" cultures to "minority" cultures. Yet, again like Kymlicka, Taylor emphasizes the cohesiveness of culture to a degree that underestimates its ambiguous boundaries. This problematic emphasis is solidified in Taylor's more recent *Modern Social Imaginaries*.[14] In this book, Taylor again gives a historical genealogy of the political principles that guide modern liberal societies. Yet here, Taylor is more interested in examining the status of these principles than their content. Are they universal? "Merely" cultural? Both? Taylor attempts to answer this question by formulating the category of "social imaginary." Taylor explains:

> By social imaginary, I mean something much broader and deeper than the intellectual schemes people may entertain when thinking about social reality in a disengaged mode. I am thinking, rather, of the ways people imagine their social existence, how they fit together with others, how things go on between them and their fellows, the expectations that are normally met, and the deeper normative notions and images that underlie these expectations.[15]

Taylor clarifies that the social imaginary is not primarily a theoretical paradigm, but deals with "the way ordinary people 'imagine' their social surroundings" which is more often "carried in images, stories, and legends," is "shared by large groups of people, if not the whole society," and "makes possible common practices and a widely shared sense of legitimacy."[16] Taylor goes on in the rest of the book to describe in great detail the particular social imaginary of "Western modernity," reiterating his earlier claim that although we can only make sense of our experience through the lens of this social imaginary, we can still attempt to "fuse horizons" with other non-Western social imaginaries. To this end, he concludes his book with a plea for "provincializing Europe" by recognizing that "our" social imaginary is only one model among many others which, we must remember from *Multiculturalism*, are deserving of the presumption of equal value.

Given that Taylor refrains from specifying his conception of culture in *Multiculturalism*, and that he returns to the central issues presented there and explains them in terms of a social imaginary, it seems reasonable to conclude that the social imaginary *is* Taylor's model of culture. Yet even (and perhaps, especially) with this specification, certain important questions remain unanswered. It is still unclear the extent to which social imaginaries are shared *within* "multicultural" societies. Taylor hints that "even within the West" there are significant differences in the development of social imaginaries (he points to his chapter on the differing courses of the French and American revolutions as evidence), but he fails to specify whether these are mere variations or different social imaginaries altogether. Moreover, Taylor's "broad and deep" conception of culture as social imaginary tends toward a troubling agnosticism. Even with the possibility of "fusing horizons" with different social imaginaries, we must still recognize the "humbling insight" that "we lack even the adequate language to describe these differences."[17] If this were true, it would be humbling indeed for those who mean to pursue political solutions to concrete problems of misrecognition and oppression. Taylor's social imaginary, like Kymlicka's conception of culture, conceals important social divisions and conflict dynamics. While it purports to recognize the unique and authentic difference of individuals, it conflates important differences among groups.

The crucial point to make clear is that this criticism of multicultural liberalism is a matter of principle and not merely of scope. Kymlicka admits as much by considering and rejecting an alternative way of justifying group rights "as a response to some disadvantage or barrier in the political process which makes it impossible for the group's views and interests to be effectively represented."[18] He attributes this position to Young, whom he quotes as claiming: "In a society where some groups are privileged while others are oppressed, insisting that as citizens persons should leave behind their particular affiliations and experiences to adopt a general point of view serves only to reinforce the privilege."[19] Kymlicka's rejection of this way of conceiving of group rights refers to the superiority of ideal theory. He claims that to conceive of rights in this way is reactionary, and that the best one could hope for would be "temporary measure[s] on the way to a society where the need for special representation no longer exists."[20] Such temporary measures must be subject to periodic reconsiderations to see if the rights are still justified. In opposition to such "political affirmative action," Kymlicka conceives of group rights in a more universal way, as "inherent" in the categories of ethnic groups and national minorities as such.[21] This defense however, underestimates the flexibility of the categories used to refer to underprivileged or oppressed groups. Even by Kymlicka's own social ontology, the status of groups is not static. "It is possible, in theory," he says, "for immigrants to become national minorities, if they settle together and acquire self-governing powers."[22] Given this admission of the historical contingency of his categories, his notion of group rights is just as subject to periodic reevaluation as a notion of group rights deriving from historical injustices.

But the differences between a liberal theory of minority cultures and theories that take seriously the concerns of oppressed groups go even deeper. In order to see how, one must understand that Kymlicka's argument for the protection of minority cultures (as well as Taylor's "politics of recognition") is derived from the liberal value of individual freedom. Kymlicka understands individual freedom as the fundamental principle of liberalism.[23] And individual freedom, he claims, is dependent upon access to a societal culture. This is because the very possibility of choosing how to live one's life requires a range of meaningful options from which to choose, which is only provided by a "shared vocabulary of tradition and convention," or what Kymlicka calls a "cultural narrative."[24] His picture of individual freedom, then, is not the picture of the isolated individual unburdened by tradition—a picture that has often been criticized by communitarians like Sandel, Walzer, Macintyre, and even Taylor—but rather that of a culturally embedded individual guiding his or her life "from the inside," choosing from a rich variety of options provided by his or her societal culture. It is important to notice, though, that this kind of argument makes cultural membership *instrumental*. It is not valuable in itself, but only insofar as it is necessary to the well-being of the individual. Cultural membership should thus count among what Rawls calls "primary goods," basic rights that any individual requires to pursue his own particular conception of a good life. Kymlicka's theory should thus be distinguished from those theories that see cultural membership as intrinsically valuable, as well as those theories that see cultural diversity as valuable to society in general.

One objection that might be made here is that Kymlicka is unrealistically optimistic about cultural membership. By focusing on the positive value of cultural membership, he may overlook its negative or limiting aspects. As Herr points out, cultural membership not only makes choice possible, but it also limits the range of choices available to culturally embedded individuals. It may be true that the societal culture of the Amish, for example, provides a range of meaningful choices for its members. But this does not preclude the criticism that this range of choices is unnecessarily narrow. An accurate picture of cultural membership must take both its enabling and limiting aspects seriously.

In a series of articles, Gerald Doppelt makes a similar point in a way that links this objection to the concern about the exclusion of relevant social groups. He argues that Kymlicka employs a "sanitized" conception of cultural identity, which leads him to overlook the negative, illiberal aspects of not only minority cultures, but dominant cultures as well. "Societal cultures," Doppelt notes, "are also the source of prejudice, discrimination, exclusion, hatred, and violence—not just between groups, but within them as well."[25] The force of this criticism, he thinks, is that group rights based on cultural identity may in fact perpetuate the very kinds of group harms that they are intended to address. Imagine, for example, a minority culture that oppresses some subgroup within its own group, say, women. For this subgroup, then, Kymlicka's justification for the protection of the minority culture will not hold up. It is not the case that the culture provides for women a range of meaningful opportunities; in fact, quite the opposite is true. Doppelt points out that "members of an oppressed subgroup within an illiberal national or ethnic minority may well be better off seeking to participate in the dominant culture, even though they may well confront discrimination and prejudice there [also]."[26]

Kymlicka does not seem to dispute this optimism about cultural identity. In a brief reply to some of his critics, he addresses the criticism that his account of group rights fails to apply to so many social groups by denouncing a "defeatism" that would presume that all relations between cultures are "inherently characterized by conflict and inequality."[27] Instead, he claims that such cases are "exceptional," and that the majority of cultural groups in fact accept the basic values of liberalism. His project, then, focuses on "successful" accommodations of cultural minorities, and he even suggests that such a focus may be applicable to the so-called exceptional cases "indirectly."[28] If it is not yet clear, I think that this presumption is deeply mistaken. In the first place, even if cultural minorities do exhibit something like the basic values of liberalism, this does not mean that their practices do not stray from these basic principles in serious, systematic ways. One need not even look to eccentric minority cultures to see such deviations from liberal principles. The dominant culture of supposedly liberal democratic states, in its employment of multidimensional structures of oppression, can demonstrate the point just as easily. But, again, the fundamental point of contention is one of substance rather than scope, and Kymlicka identifies it clearly in his reply. Theories of cultural minority deny, as Kymlicka does, that "conflict and inequality" are central features of the organization of social groups. Theories of oppression, on the other hand, see conflict as constitutive of group formation. Additionally, the methodology of theories of oppression takes groups as fundamental in their social ontology, as opposed to multicultural liberalism's methodological individualism, which I have begun to demonstrate above. Let me now turn to these points and explain these fundamental differences in more detail.

THEORIES OF OPPRESSION

In the same reply discussed above, Kymlicka sets the parameters for evaluating his own theory. He asserts that "the only way to defend my approach . . . is to show that alternative approaches have even greater costs in terms of our moral ideals."[29] This is a difficult task, he maintains, primarily because there are not enough alternatives with which to contrast his own. Theories of oppression, I will argue, represent just such an alternative. In what follows, I will present the main points of contrast and show that theories of oppression are superior, both in terms of their explanatory power and in terms of "our" moral ideals.

Multiculturalism pictures cultures as organic, self-contained, self-sufficient, and relatively isolated from one another. The idea one gets from such a view is that under normal circumstances cultures flourish side by side, coming into conflict only when there is not enough room, so to speak, for more than one of them (for example, government business, education, and so on must be undertaken in some language or another). But such conflicts appear as departures from the norm, the inevitable consequence of squeezing several cultures into a limited space. Theories of oppression, on the other hand, are agonistic. That is, they assert the fundamentality of *conflict* for understanding the reality of social groups. Oppressed groups exist in relation to one or more oppressor groups, which in turn define themselves in contrast to the groups they oppress. Unlike the concept of culture, the concept of oppression is a *relational* concept.

The locus classicus of this alternative view is Marx, whose critique of classical liberalism's avoidance of class conflict remains influential and informative. Marx, following Hegel, criticized liberalism for a social ontology that saw individuals, unencumbered by social relations, as the fundamental agents of political economy. For Marx, this individualism concealed the fact that society is divided into classes based upon the individual's relation to the means of production. A system of bourgeois rights that aims to secure political emancipation not only leaves this more fundamental group-based injustice untouched, it serves, ideologically, to conceal and reproduce it. In other words, liberalism's failure to understand (or acknowledge) the ways in which a certain kind of social group structures liberal capitalist societies serves to entrench a certain kind of group harm—exploitation—even as it purports to eliminate certain fundamental individual harms. The insistence upon individual freedom actually conceals a basic unfreedom premised upon one's group membership, and the insistence on equality among individuals actually conceals a basic inequality among classes. Thus Marx professes to give an *immanent critique* of liberalism, based upon its own values of freedom and equality.

Though Marxism generally has been widely criticized, rightly and wrongly, in ways that it is not my concern to analyze, it is undeniable that the Marxist critique of liberal individualism has made possible analogous critiques of other kinds of group-based harm, which focus on social groups other than class, such as race, gender, and so on.

Charles Mills's account of white supremacy is an example of such an analogous immanent critique and a paradigmatic theory of oppression. Mills provides a systematic explanation of the perpetuation of racial oppression alongside liberal principles of freedom and equality that would appear to condemn such a phenomenon. Unlike the common liberal response, which understands racial inequality as an unfortunate departure from nonetheless admirable liberal ideals, Mills shows how the fundamental principles of liberalism are *symbiotic* with the continued existence of racial oppression.[30] Racial oppression can coexist with liberal principles of individual freedom and equality because the development of these principles was actually premised upon the previous exclusion of nonwhites. The enshrinement of individual rights and freedoms, then, and the supposedly universal and abstract justification of those rights and freedoms conceal the fact that only certain kinds of individuals, whites, could be considered bearers of individual rights deserving of equal treatment. In fact, it is this very feature of white (male) persons that is supposed to distinguish them from nonwhite subpersons and thus establish their superiority and "civilization" as opposed to the inferior nonwhite "savage," who lives in a perpetual state of nature, and lacks the rationality necessary to escape this brutal state.[31] Traditional liberalism, then, actually employs a dual normative standard—one set of rules for whites and another for nonwhites. Thus the continued inequality and oppression of nonwhite peoples is not a "deviation" from liberal norms, but in fact adheres to the dual standards of a "racial liberalism."[32]

Mills's theory clearly exhibits the key features of a theory of oppression as I have identified them. Liberal individualism, it claims, actually obscures a more fundamental group-based racial ontology, the division of human beings into white and nonwhite, and the privileging of the one over the other. This group-based account of white supremacy will look very different from individualist accounts. The latter tend to psychologize racism, understanding it as a psychological aberration that must be eliminated through education, therapy, and so on. Mills echoes this point: "The attitudinal and atomistic, individualist focus of at least some varieties of liberalism," he points out, "reduces the issue to bigotry, which needs to be purged through moral exhortation."[33] Individualist approaches will thus miss important systematic and structural features of white supremacy that would persist even if everyone adopted a properly tolerant attitude. This is because the apologist for the racial polity can always point to some successful nonwhite individual, and conclude from this that it is possible to succeed, and that those who have not must have not because of their own personal moral failings: laziness, lack of motivation, and so on. Likewise, the apologist can point to white individuals who face serious obstacles and systematic disadvantages that (they assume) are at least as bad as those faced by nonwhites. These assumptions are clearly debatable, but my intention is not to debate them. The point is that the very enterprise of comparing and contrasting individual successes and failures has no bearing on the claim that whites *as a group* are privileged and nonwhites *as a group* are oppressed. Such a claim is perfectly consistent with a few black Horatio Algers (or Barack Obamas) and a few whites at the bottom of the barrel.

Mills's theory also takes conflict as fundamental. He suggests "conceptualizing personhood as a battlefield, a terrain of political contestation."[34] This allows groups categorized by racial liberalism as "subpersons" to assert their full humanity. It remains an open question, and one much discussed in black political theory, whether this fight to be seen, finally, as a full person ought to lead to integration into the dominant social, legal, and political structures, or whether separate institutional structures are warranted. Kymlicka and other multicultural liberals may be helpful for thinking about these issues, but not without first taking existing racial divisions seriously and recognizing the deep, constitutive conflict that they generate within racialized societies. In other words, a multiculturalism that took race seriously would look much more like a theory of oppression, and it would provide a very different picture of social reality, as I will now begin to show.

I argued above that Kymlicka's multicultural liberalism conceals integration problems in groups that do not fall under his very stringent category of minority cultures, and that understanding cultures the way he does leads him to overlook important differences among those who supposedly share the same "cultural" institutions. Mills's analysis of immigration illustrates this in a particularly poignant way. Mills agrees with Kymlicka that immigration policy long employed an assimilationist ideal. Yet, Mills notes that what immigrants must assimilate to is not (or not only) the dominant culture, but the *existing racial dichotomy*. So, upon arrival to the United States, for example, some immigrants are deemed "white" without further review. Others, like Italians, Irish, and especially Jews, were "whites with a question mark" or "probationary whites."[35] Those ethnic groups that achieve "whiteness" are integrated, while those that do not remain segregated. Further, those that are not integrated often begin to have more in common with Kymlicka's description of national minorities. They retain cultural, if not legal autonomy, by being involuntarily segregated in urban areas in which they form a majority. They often speak little English, retaining their native language not necessarily by choice, but as a result of inadequate resources for linguistic integration. It is not surprising, then, that residential segregation is a feature common to both "ethnic groups" in Kymlicka's sense, and nonwhites. For Mills the two categories are mutually inclusive, at least insofar as race is subsumed theoretically under ethnicity.[36] Ethnic groups that are decided to be nonwhite are excluded from the white polity, while ethnic groups that have been deemed "white" are integrated in much the way Kymlicka describes ethnic groups as such. This illustrates both the danger of essentializing disadvantaged groups, and the fungibility of Kymlicka's social categories.

Kymlicka also overlooks important differences among groups he describes as national minorities. Kymlicka's clearest examples of national minorities are the Quebecois in Canada, and Native Americans in the United States and Canada. As national minorities, he argues that these groups ought to enjoy some self-government rights, as well as weighted input upon issues in the majority culture that adversely affect them. According to Kymlicka, this is already true of these two groups, albeit in a limited way. So, for the first example, the francophone province of Quebec, Kymlicka says it "has extensive jurisdiction over issues that are crucial to the survival of the French culture, including control over education, language, culture, as well as significant input into immigration policy."[37] In this case, national minorities are accommodated through federalism. For Native Americans, however,

> self-government has been primarily tied to the system of reserved lands . . . Substantial powers have been devolved from the federal government to the tribal/band councils which govern each reserve. Indian tribes/bands have been acquiring increasing control over health, education, family law, policing, criminal justice, and resource development. They are becoming, in effect, a third order of government.[38]

Though it may be truer in Canada (in the corresponding footnote, Kymlicka gives only the Canadian example of the Inuit as evidence of his claim), to say that tribal reservations in the United States are becoming "a third order of government" is misleading at best. Though in recent years steps have been taken to give special rights to indigenous groups (exclusive licenses to run casinos, for example), Native Americans remain the poorest minority in the United States. Control over resources on indigenous lands has led to a continuation of the policies of "Indian removal" which are older than the United States itself.

Describing indigenous peoples as self-governing national minorities allows the majority culture to shirk its responsibility to acknowledge and respond to the vast inequalities that are the result of historical injustices committed against the minority culture, injustices usually committed in the name of racial superiority. Further, by euphemistically describing national minorities as "previously self-governing," Kymlicka conflates two very different historical processes: conquest and confederation. The case of Quebec is a case of one dominant white European power accommodating the culture of another through federalism. The case of Native Americans is a case of white

Europeans decimating the culture of a nonwhite people and placing (often by force) the small remainder of them in reservations. The ignorance of issues of race in this context leads Kymlicka to overlook the important fact that the reservation system was not implemented in order to accommodate the self-government rights of a minority culture, but was more comparable to a concentration camp in which a people deemed racially inferior were forcibly relocated according to the convenience of the "master race."

Finally, a raceless account of cultural minorities misses not only important differences, but important commonalities as well. Kymlicka points out that the category of "Hispanic" actually conflates many different issues and individuals. Some individuals counted as Hispanic meet his definition of national minorities (Puerto Ricans, Chicanos, and perhaps Cuban exiles). Others fall under his definition of ethnic groups (most other voluntary immigrants from Latin America). Kymlicka further points out that individual members of these groups often do not self-identify as Hispanic but as Puerto Rican, Mexican, Ecuadorian, and so on.[39] Certainly Kymlicka is right about all this, and one should be cautious about ascribing artificial social categories to groups that do not self-identify with them. But what Kymlicka misses is that these various groups do have at least one thing in common. They are, at least in the context of the United States and its system of racial classification, most often grouped together and classed as nonwhite, such that they face some of the same barriers and disadvantages as other racial minorities and some that are unique to "Hispanics" (such as the presumption that all people of Latin American descent are in the United States illegally). Even though the categorization might be artificial (as is the category of race itself), it still has very real consequences for those it purports to describe. Thus Kymlicka precludes any sort of political affinity around Hispanic identity, and non-whiteness generally, a phenomenon that could combat the unjust advantages of whiteness and systematic racism.

Further, the shortcomings of a purely individualist approach to identifying and remedying group-based disadvantages (cultural or otherwise) can be made in a more general way. In *The Reality of Social Groups*, Paul Sheehy demonstrates the inadequacy of individualism alone for explaining important social phenomena. Explanations that reference groups causally are fairly common. Consider the following example. In Seattle in 1999, massive protests virtually shut down the third ministerial conference of the World Trade Organization. By taking control of key intersections, and also by sheer number, protestors made it impossible for WTO delegates to reach the conference destination. Setting aside issues of the morality of tactics, the events just described cannot even be explained, let alone evaluated, on an individualist model. It is true that the group was comprised of several thousand *individuals*. Yet this fact is inadequate at best and irrelevant at worst to the explanation of the events. The actions of the group cannot be reduced, in this case, to the actions and/or intentions of its individual members. Sheehy writes that "if the joint action is broken down into its individual components, then the essential element in its effectiveness is lost—the jointness or coordination of the actions."[40] An individual, however determined, cannot by mere presence make a street inaccessible, breach a barricade, or halt factory production. Such effects must include the group qua group among its causes. In such cases, the collective nature of the group is irreducible.

The same can be said also for group harms. An individual can be harmed in a number of direct ways: through acts of violence, discrimination, humiliation, and so on. But groups can also be the irreducible objects of harm. Hate crimes, for example, take the form of individual harms, but are additionally, and even primarily, group harms. A person attacked in virtue of their race, gender, or sexuality is obviously harmed individually. But other members of her group can also be said to be harmed, even though the attack was not aimed at them individually. The lynching of African Americans, for example, is an attack on blacks as a whole, and not just the individual victims. This is part of the justification underlying harsher penalties for crimes that target individuals based upon their group memberships.[41] Further, it is not just the threat of potential harm to other like individuals that justifies saying that they are harmed. A Hmong woman living in a Western democracy may have no reason to fear individual mistreatment based on reports that Hmong people are being mistreated elsewhere, but she may still be harmed emotionally or otherwise by the fact that members of her group have suffered because of their group membership.

Sheehy's criticisms of pure individualism illuminate the reasons why a theory based on such a methodology tends to overlook conflict, instead imagining and overestimating cooperation, voluntary interaction, and consent. Multicultural liberalism takes voluntary association as the paradigm of group membership. If it didn't, then it couldn't understand the value of group membership in terms of primary goods: things *individuals* pursue as part of their vision of a worthwhile life. Whether one focuses on the enabling conditions of group membership as a context for meaningful choices, or on its limiting conditions, the focus remains on the individual—the extent to which he or she chooses to associate with other individuals, and the effects of this choice on his or her other choices. Such an understanding of groups—call it *intentionalism*—tends to overlook groups that are formed by forces outside of the individual's control, or at least, sees such groups as anomalous, and oppressed groups fit precisely this definition, as I will now argue.

DEFINING OPPRESSION

Oppression should be understood as a group harm of the type Sheehy identifies. In a brief but informative essay, Marilyn Frye defines oppression in a similar way. "If an individual is oppressed," she asserts, "it is in virtue of being a member of a group or category of people that is systematically reduced, molded, immobilized. Thus, to recognize a person as oppressed, one has to see that individual *as* belonging to a group of a certain sort."[42] Accordingly, she makes a similar distinction between individual and group harm. She imagines a "rich white playboy" who breaks a leg in a skiing accident. Clearly such a person is harmed, but he is not oppressed, she claims, even if his injury can be traced to someone's negligence or intentional malice.[43] Even violations of fundamental individual rights do not automatically translate to instances of oppression. If the government seizes my property, for example, or denies my right to freedom of speech, this violation should not automatically be characterized as oppression. If, however, the government seizes the property of, or denies the right to free speech of a certain group, based solely or primarily on preexisting group membership, then the violation is properly called an instance of oppression. When oppression is used loosely to name any and all forms of harm and human suffering, it loses much of its critical potential. Oppression points to a phenomenon that may include individual harm, but is nonetheless analytically distinct from it.

But this definition is not yet precise enough. Must we count the mandatory registration of sex offenders, for example, as an instance of oppression? If sex offenders count as a social group, and if this restriction is placed upon them in virtue of being a member of that group, then it seems we must. If this seems intuitively problematic, it is because the idea that oppressed groups are social groups of a "certain sort" has not yet been specified clearly enough. The key to specifying this further condition, as suggested above, lies in the rejection of intentionalism. Oppressed groups are paradigmatically non-intentional. That is, they do not depend upon, and generally do without, the voluntary consent of their members. The existence of a racial group, for example, does not depend upon the identification of a shared purpose on the part of those it purports to classify. Instead, these groupings are often understood as somehow "natural."[44] But sex offenders, difficult questions of nature versus nurture aside, are grouped together based upon some individual criminal action(s) that they committed. So though they might not share a common purpose in any robust sense, they still count as an intentional group, given that society has seen fit to aggregate their actions together in a way that defines them as a group.

In other words, they share a characteristic that is deemed socially relevant in an important way. But individuals can share other socially relevant features besides individual actions and intentions. They can share *external* characteristics, like social disadvantage, and these also bind individuals together as social groups. In *Analyzing Oppression*, Ann Cudd focuses on these latter features in attempting to define oppressed groups.[45] She argues against those who claim that social groups are necessarily defined by shared intentions. Many relevant social groups do not meet this qualification, particularly oppressed groups. But what, then, qualifies an oppressed group as a group? For her, the key feature is shared social constraints. She explains that constraints are social "when they come about as a result of social actions," including "legal rights, obligations and burdens, stereotypical expectations, wealth, income, social status, conventions, norms, and practices."[46] Such constraints can and do shape intentional as much as non-intentional groups, as the sex offender example illustrates, but oppression proper occurs when these constraints are based upon non-voluntary group membership.

Social groups do not always fit neatly into this dichotomy, however. In reality, they are often shaped by both intentional and non-intentional forces. Consider, for example, Jews. As a social group, Jews are defined in reference to both intentional and non-intentional characteristics: in terms of religious belief and in terms of race. One may not practice Judaism but still be considered Jewish either by self-identification or ascription. And one may not be Jewish "by birth," but convert to Judaism and come to see oneself as a Jew, and be so seen by others as well. The question of what, if anything, makes one "really" Jewish is irrelevant here.[47] The point is that oppression aims to eliminate this complexity, deemphasizing or eliminating intentional aspects of group membership, and attempting to demarcate group membership completely non-intentionally. The practice of forcing Jews and other minorities to wear special identifying badges, founded in medieval Islam and Christianity and adopted by the Third Reich, illustrates this tendency in one of its starkest forms. And while greater phenotypical differences tend to make such a practice unnecessary for racial classifications in the United States, other standards, such as the so-called "one drop rule," achieve the same effect.[48]

Of course, such a process is rarely if ever completely successful. Movements against oppression often take the form of redefining group identity by reintroducing and emphasizing elements of intentionality. This involves not only replacing perceived negative characteristics of group membership with positive ones ("black is beautiful," and so on), but revealing how the very construction of the group is based upon human convention rather than natural fact. Thus the movement to recognize group membership as "socially constructed" allows gender benders, race traitors, and others to make voluntary choices about membership where previously choice was thought (or made to appear) impossible. But it does not follow from the fact that oppression never completely eliminates intentional aspects of group membership that oppression does not necessarily involve the attempt to do so. The movement to eliminate intentional features of group membership is a necessary condition for oppression.

But is it also a sufficient condition? That is, does the attempt to eliminate intentionality lead in all cases to oppression? Superficially, it seems that it does not. Certain kinds of groups might be thought to be non-intentional but not necessarily oppressed. Consider the group of people with green eyes. Here is a group based upon a nonvoluntary characteristic, but one that is probably not oppressed, at least not in virtue of this specific characteristic. But such a group does not really count as a *social* group, because the characteristic of having green eyes is not normally deemed socially relevant. The group is a "series," to use Sartre's term: a mere aggregate. Now, if green-eyed persons came to be thought of as less intelligent, or somehow less "pure" than other groups, and were, further, subject to harm based on their group membership, then the characteristic *would* become socially relevant, and we ought to consider the group of green-eyed persons oppressed.[49]

Let us consider a more difficult case, the case of oppressor groups. On what basis can we distinguish these groups from the groups that they oppress? If, as has been said, oppression is a kind of group harm involving the attempt to eliminate intentional aspects of group membership, then one might claim (and some have claimed) that oppressor groups are themselves oppressed. After all, in a racially categorized society, whiteness is just as nonvoluntary as blackness. And in a gendered society, maleness is just as nonvoluntary as femaleness.[50] Further, whites, males, and other individual members of oppressor groups may experience their membership as a social constraint. Perhaps a man has a difficult time pursuing a career that has traditionally been associated with women, or a white person is harassed for moving into a predominantly black neighborhood. To see how oppressor groups are distinct from the groups they oppress, one must appreciate the distinction between individual and group harm.

One could make a case that non-intentional social groupings are unjust in general, insofar as they place restrictions on individual autonomy. One's social group ought to have no bearing on the opportunities available to him or her, whether or not that group is oppressed. In fact, such an argument is central to liberal individualism and provides the justification for many of the civil and political rights enshrined in liberal democracies. However, the key to distinguishing oppressor and oppressed groups is that the social constraints imposed upon the former do not harm the group qua group, even if they do constrain individual members of that group in certain ways. In fact, quite the opposite is true. In general, the constraints imposed upon individual members of oppressor groups are *beneficial* to the group as a whole. Categorizing certain sectors of the workforce as "women's work" preserves better, higher paid sectors for men, reduces competition in those sectors, and so on. Consider Frye's example:

> The boundaries of a racial ghetto in an American city serve to some extent to keep white people from going in, as well as to keep ghetto dwellers from going out. A particular white citizen may be frustrated or feel deprived because s/he cannot stroll around there and enjoy the "exotic" aura of a "foreign" culture, or shop for bargains in the ghetto swap shops. In fact, the existence of the ghetto, or racial segregation, does deprive the white person of knowledge and harm her/his character by nurturing unwarranted feelings of superiority. But this does not make the white person in this situation a member of an oppressed race . . . [the barrier] is a product of the intention, planning and action of whites for the benefit of whites, to secure and maintain privileges that are available to whites generally, as members of the dominant and privileged group . . . This barrier is not oppressive to whites, even though it is a barrier to whites.[51]

The non-intentionality of group membership alone, then, is not sufficient to demonstrate oppression. The elimination of intentionality must lead to group harm. It is not surprising that liberal multiculturalism misses this distinction, since it fails to see groups as separate from the individuals who comprise them, and so fails to distinguish between individual and group harm. Without this distinction, one may recognize that the harms caused by certain kinds social constraints differ in degree (perhaps racial minorities, women, etc., experience them more frequently, or more intensely), but one will miss that they are fundamentally different kinds of harms. And since it is in part group harm that characterizes oppression, the very category of oppressed group will not seem to be a sound ontological category from that perspective.

Not all accounts of oppression take groups as fundamental. Some accounts aim to extend the term oppression to (or even reserve it for) certain individual harms. Sally Haslanger, for example, distinguishes structural oppression, which is what I have offered an account of above, from "agent oppression."[52] She understands the latter simply enough as an individual agent "misusing their power to harm another."[53] Under this description, oppression is fundamentally an issue of individual moral wrongdoing. One who reserves the term oppression for *only* this type of harm must maintain that structures or institutions either cannot be oppressive, or can be only in a derivative sense, insofar as they embody the oppressive intentions of individual agents.[54] Haslanger rightly notes that this conception alone is inadequate, in the first place because the complexity of institutions and practices often prevents or makes irrelevant the identification of some individual agent responsible for their effects. For her part, then, Haslanger recommends a "mixed" approach, which would apply the term oppression to both structural and individual instances.

In my view, such a "mixed" approach is too broad, and fails to distinguish oppression from immoral acts in general. If oppression is simply a case of one individual harming another, then virtually all (or at least a great deal of) immoral actions will count as oppression. If a valet misuses his or her "power" to steal my car, then the valet oppresses me. A paperboy (or girl) who intentionally breaks my window (perhaps I am a particularly ill-tempered customer) oppresses me. A stranger who assaults me arbitrarily oppresses me. Such uses of the term oppression seem misused, and stretch, devalue, and water down the meaning of the term, which ought to remain a powerful name for a serious and systematic normative failure. As Haslanger herself notes, "unless more can be said about *unjust* action as distinct from *immoral* action, oppression would just collapse into wrongful harm."[55]

Secondly, power, on any understanding of the term that goes beyond mere physical force, is itself structurally distributed, such that the ability to misuse one's power is itself related to one's position in a complex web of social arrangements. Consider Haslanger's example: She imagines a bigoted professor who consistently gives low grades to women of color, regardless of their performance. Such women, Haslanger thinks, are *not* structurally oppressed, though they may nonetheless be individually oppressed by the professor's bad behavior.[56] Yet, given my definition above, what is really oppressive about such a case is that certain individuals (women of color in Professor X's class) are being harmed *because of* their membership in a certain group (women, nonwhites, or both). This membership is nonvoluntary, and is constructed by processes outside of both the students' and the professor's control. Thus the very ability of the professor to "oppress" certain of his or her students is determined by a preexisting social arrangement that is itself oppressive. Thus the women of color students *are* structurally oppressed, and the professor's actions are an instance of that oppression.

Finally, even if one does make the important distinction between unjust and immoral acts, one should make distinctions among kinds of injustice as well. I would hesitate, for example, to use oppression as an umbrella concept to capture what is wrong with a variety of injustices. For example, Iris Marion Young suggests that oppression includes at least five different forms of injustice: exploitation, marginalization, powerlessness, cultural imperialism, and systematic violence.[57] Again, such an approach (which is otherwise insightful and illuminating, especially in linking oppression to group identification) risks conflating too many different phenomena, bringing oppression ever closer to a kind of empty signifier, used and (by some) abused to name every kind of harm a group can suffer. I doubt, for example, that *any* single concept can capture what is going on in, say, the structure of wage-labor under a capitalist mode of production as well as the devaluation of traditional forms of life in underdeveloped postcolonial nations, as well as the use of mass rape as a genocidal strategy in regions marred by war and ethnic violence. For this reason, my definition of oppression is intentionally narrow, and, though it may be somewhat stipulative, it nonetheless captures the sense of oppression most relevant to contemporary liberal democracies.

NORMATIVE INTENTIONALISM

I have argued that an intentionalist account of group membership, to which multicultural liberalism subscribes at least implicitly, is inadequate as a foundation of group rights, not least because it fails to recognize oppressed groups. Such an oversight is unacceptable insofar as oppressed groups represent (or at least ought to represent) one of the most normatively pressing concerns for supposedly liberal democracies. Now whether or not intentionalism about groups is desirable *as a normative goal* remains to be seen. One might think that group membership *ought* to be based solely on voluntary association, and that groups formed by coercion or other external forces are somehow illegitimate. But multicultural liberalism does not make this claim explicit. Rather it commits the fallacy of presuming that what ought to be (if indeed it ought to be) already is. And so non-intentional groups fall off of its radar and are treated only peripherally, if it all. One should not forget, however, that the task of political philosophy is not only to accurately diagnose injustices, but, perhaps more importantly, to suggest ways in which they might be remedied. For the latter task, intentionalism deserves further consideration.

Carol Gould recognizes many of the shortcomings of multicultural liberalism noted above and tries nonetheless to develop a normatively intentionalist account of group rights that takes cultures as its fundamental units. She too begins with an analysis of racial oppression and multicultural liberalism's failure to address it. She notes that the problem with racial identity is that it is "ascriptive" (her term for non-intentional). "Here," she argues, "the basis for membership in the group is not common purposes or shared understandings, but rather the objective circumstance of being put in a particular situation of oppression not by choice."[58] Ascriptive identities of this sort do not mesh well with the democratic ideals of freedom and equality. The normative goals of democratic politics should then include "the freedom to shape one's group identity with others and to develop multiple group identities, where the criterial features—bodily or otherwise—are open to continuous interpretation and choice."[59] In other words, the goal is to "move to self-ascription."[60] This ideal is central to what she calls "inclusive intercultural democracy."

Interestingly, Gould chooses to understand normatively justifiable group identity in terms of culture. "The concept of culture," she says, "has the advantage of being more open and more fully free than the alternatives of 'race,' 'ethnicity,' and 'nationality.'"[61] Presuming that this is true (and that is no small presumption),[62] it is difficult to see why only these alternatives are relevant, or why a general account of groups could not do the philosophical work that Gould requires of culture. At any rate, it is surprising that Gould specifies her normative conception in this way, given her many reservations about the use of culture in multiculturalist discourse. She notes in several places that understanding groups in cultural terms risks "reification" by overlooking important differences and establishing false commonalities.[63] Accordingly, she criticizes Kymlicka, Taylor, and others for employing a conception of culture that is too strong and encompassing. She distinguishes her own looser conception of culture, which acknowledges that "there is a wide range of highly significant culturally defined groups that lie outside this strong definition of culture."[64] Her focus, then, is cultural identity in this weaker sense, which allows that individuals may identify with more than one culture, and denies that cultural membership requires the kind of infrastructure that makes it "societal" in Kymlicka's sense.

Still, like Kymlicka, Taylor, and others, she sees culture primarily as "a condition for the agency of individuals," and derives the rights of cultural groups ultimately from the rights of its individual members.[65] So, despite her concerns for oppressed groups, she must ultimately admit that oppressed groups "are not simply characterizable as cultural minorities," though she does think that the two categories "overlap" insofar as some cultural minorities are also oppressed.[66] This makes oppression a secondary concern, and she argues rather simply that a "parallel case" can be made for group rights for oppressed groups, based upon the same interpretation of freedom and equality that undergirds her conception of cultural rights.

Yet more so than Kymlicka, Taylor, and other multicultural liberals, Gould's general normative strategy is informative. If oppression is marked by non-intentionality, then the mitigation of oppression must make self-ascription possible. That is, groups must be free to develop their own interpretations of their collective identity, without coercion or external constraint. This, I will argue, is a fundamental right that groups possess: formulated positively, *a right to self-ascription*; formulated negatively (but amounting to the same thing), *a right not to be oppressed*. Such a right requires specification. It implies that understanding group rights requires understanding group identity. Further, a conception of group identity that can sustain a theory of group rights must be normative. That is, it must tell us how groups would or ought to construct their collective identity in a (more) just society. Initially, this claim may sound frighteningly tyrannical. I do not mean to give an account of what certain groups should be like, since this marks precisely the kind of coercive, ascriptive, nonvoluntary process that I aim to condemn. I do mean to give an account of what it would look like for groups to be able to freely construct their own identity, and what sort of social and political framework would be most conducive to such processes.

In other words, my account will be, in part, procedural. Accordingly, I draw inspiration from the work of Jürgen Habermas, in particular his theory of communicative action, which grounds rationality in the intersubjective structure of communication; as well as his discourse ethic, which shows how such a communicative intersubjectivity gives rise to universally binding norms. Though his theoretical aims are much more ambitious and far-reaching than mine—purporting to reconstruct a new and foundational form of rationality as well as a renewed foundation for morality in general—I will argue that his theories provide insight also into the process of constructing group identity, and can provide a clue as to how one might give a normative account of group identity without ascribing to a substantive account of what groups must be like. More specifically, I will argue that his central claims about how moral utterances can be normatively justified can be modified to apply to the process of negotiating collective identity, a claim he has touched upon in various places but never systematically developed.

I have argued that oppression cannot be understood in terms of individual harm, and so we should not expect it to be remedied by individual rights. Since oppression involves harm to the group qua group, then group rights that aim to alleviate it must also attach to the group itself, not just as a shorthand way of referring to certain kinds of individual rights. To acknowledge this is not to deny the existence of individual rights, nor even to say that group rights are in all cases primary. Nor does the existence of cases where group rights conflict with individual rights justify the rejection of one or the other, any more than the existence of ethical dilemmas in general justifies the rejection of the duties or principles that they show to be conflicting. Such cases cannot be decided in a general way, though I will try to give some guidelines for resolving them in the following chapters. I do mean to suggest that, *in order to understand and address oppression*, groups and group rights must be understood as fundamental and irreducible. This is why I claim that theories of oppression are essentially different from liberal theories of cultural minority, not as complementary approaches to understanding overlapping social categories, but as competing theoretical frameworks for understanding group-based injustices. What's more, I take these competing frameworks to be incommensurable with one another, for reasons I will now make explicit.

Though certain groups may in fact be understood as both oppressed groups and cultural groups (and so the term "oppressed culture" is not meaningless), when rights are attributed to such a group they are attributed *either* in virtue of their culture-hood, as providing a range of meaningful individual choices, and so forth, *or* in virtue of their oppression, as a response to a certain kind of group harm. I suspect that most often, it is in virtue of their oppression that the question of group rights becomes most pressing.[67] If this is true, then an account of group rights based upon a theory of oppression will be more fruitful than theories based upon the values of cultural membership, not only because it can deal with cases that multiculturalism fails to address, but also because it gives a more accurate picture of the cases that multiculturalism *does* address. In other words, to reiterate, a theory of oppression, including a theory of rights for oppressed groups, is not just a supplement to or "parallel case" of a theory of group rights based upon cultural membership. It is an alternative theory, and a superior one, for the moral and epistemological reasons noted above.

One may object, however, to the very desirability of a normatively intentional account. Michael Walzer argues, for example, that "the ideal picture of autonomous individuals choosing their connections (and disconnections) without restraints of any sort is an example of bad utopianism."[68] He argues that generalizing the value of voluntary association to all human associations is sociologically naive and philosophically suspect. Some associations, he thinks, are simply nonvoluntary, and (what is the more important claim here) that this fact is perhaps unavoidable and not necessarily morally or politically egregious. He thus concludes that "freedom requires nothing more than the possibility of breaking involuntary bonds and, furthermore, that the actual break is not always a good thing, and that we need not always make it easy."[69] In support of this conclusion, Walzer points out that our associational life is constrained in a variety of ways: by the kinds of families, cultures, and political structures we are born into, by the forms of association that are socially available, and by the rules of morality. In other words, he posits a "radical givenness" of our associational possibilities, and argues that this givenness is morally justifiable in that without it "society itself would be unimaginable."[70]

It seems to me that Walzer is right about this radical givenness. Of course individuals are born and socialized into certain associations, traditions, and practices. Taken to the extreme, one could deduce from such constraints that *none* of our choices, associational or otherwise, are voluntary, since they are always conditioned by a variety of factors outside of our control. Still, there are important distinctions to be made. Race, gender, and other ascriptive categories are involuntary in a much stronger sense than political affiliation, religion, citizenship, and so on. In a society like ours, there is little or no possibility of "breaking [those] involuntary bonds." Indeed, the fact that Walzer admits that the *possibility* of exiting involuntary associations (and identities) must be retained is itself a kind of weak voluntarism (or as I prefer, normative intentionalism), since *completely* involuntary associations are for the most part *impossible* to leave.[71] One does not need to imagine individuals completely unencumbered by social, political, and cultural ties in order to argue that, ideally, groups (including associations and identity groups) ought to be voluntary, at least in a weak sense like the one Walzer himself expresses.

To the contrary, my account of self-ascription, as the reader will see, begins from a similar kind of social embeddedness. It begins, that is, with groups, rather than individuals, as I have argued that any account which aims to understand and remediate oppression must. Whatever else might be said against such an approach, it is clearly not the target of Walzer's critique. Rather, as becomes apparent toward the end of his essay, the real target of his critique is a certain kind of postmodernism that sees the construction of identity and association as a project for *individuals*, a kind of "self-fashioning," to use the term Walzer attributes to Julia Kristeva, George Kateb, and similar thinkers.[72] Yet this is only one interpretation of the claim that identities are "socially constructed" and not, I will argue, the best one. Unlike these accounts, I do not advocate (or imagine) that a just society must eliminate *all* constraints on association and identity formation, only those that are oppressive, as noted above. A normatively intentional account that acknowledges the inevitability of some constraints, and takes groups rather than individuals as the fundamental agents of (collective) identity ascription, avoids Walzer's objections to individualistic voluntarism.

Finally, it is necessary to address the criticism that the normative intentionalist approach I have described marks a return to the very ideal theory that Kymlicka invokes to defend his focus on minority cultures, and so perhaps suffers from the same oversights that ideal theory is especially prone to. Recall that Kymlicka rejects conceiving of group rights "as a response to some disadvantage or barrier in the political process" on the grounds that such rights are at best temporary, and so amount to a kind of "political affirmative action" that fails to address the deeper issue of accommodating cultural minorities.[73] I have argued, to the contrary, that freedom from oppression is central to the accommodation of groups in general, including cultural groups. This is a crucial point for understanding why theories of oppression and theories of cultural minority are *competing* rather than complementary or analogous theories. The attempt to eliminate intentionality leading to group harm (that is, oppression), is precisely what is at issue in cases where accommodating cultural minorities becomes problematic. That is, it is not minority cultures *simpliciter*, but oppressed minority cultures that deserve to be considered as candidates for special rights or accommodations. Therefore, a theory of oppression is necessary for properly understanding even the paradigm cases of group rights based upon cultural membership.

In other words, ideal theory is not in itself objectionable. It is even unavoidable insofar as all normative theory is in some sense ideal. What is objectionable is an ideal theory that idealizes in such a way that certain problems can no longer be addressed within its mechanisms of abstraction; a theory that makes certain "nonideal" problems disappear. Oppression represents such a problem, and one should not be satisfied with a theory of group rights that abstracts it away as if by magic, with a few conciliatory remarks. Alternatively, a responsible social theory must take stock of the situation "on the ground." More specifically, a normative account of group identity must be informed by how groups actually do construct their identity. This is why Habermas is useful, since his normative theory is grounded in a certain way in actually existing communicative practice. Further reflections on this link between ideal discourse and the actual preconditions of communication will serve to clarify the link between ideal and nonideal theory. That is, what follows will be an attempt at a more responsible ideal theory.

NOTES

1. See, for example, Michael Sandel, *Liberalism and the Limits of Justice* (Cambridge: Cambridge University Press, 1998); Alistair Macintyre, *Whose Justice? Which Rationality?* (Notre Dame, IN: University of Notre Dame Press, 1988); Michael Walzer, *Spheres of Justice* (Oxford: Blackwell, 1983); and Charles Taylor, *Sources of the Self: The Making of Modern Identity* (Cambridge: Cambridge University Press, 1989).
2. See, for example, Will Kymlicka, "Do We Need a Liberal Theory of Minority Rights? Reply to Carens, Young, Parekh and Forst." *Constellations* 4, no. 1 (1997): 72-87.
3. Ranjoo Seodu Herr, "Liberal Multiculturalism: An Oxymoron?" *The Philosophical Forum* 38 no. 1 (2007): 23-41.
4. Kymlicka, *Multicultural Citizenship*. 10.
5. Kymlicka, *Multicultural Citizenship*. 24.
6. Kymlicka, *Multicultural Citizenship*. 19.
7. Iris Marion Young, "Polity and Group Difference: A Critique of the Ideal of Universal Citizenship." *Ethics* 99, no. 2 (1989): 250-74.
8. Kymlicka, *Multicultural Citizenship*. 76.
9. Kymlicka, *Multicultural Citizenship*. 80.
10. Kymlicka, *Multicultural Citizenship*. 77.
11. Charles Taylor et al., *Multiculturalism: Examining the Politics of Recognition*. edited by Amy Gutmann (Princeton, NJ: Princeton University Press, 1994).
12. Taylor, *Multiculturalism*. 67.
13. Taylor, *Multiculturalism*. 63.
14. Charles Taylor, *Modern Social Imaginaries* (Durham, NC: Duke University Press, 2004).
15. Taylor, *Modern Social Imaginaries*. 23.
16. Taylor, *Modern Social Imaginaries*. 23.
17. Taylor, *Modern Social Imaginaries*. 196.
18. Kymlicka, *Multicultural Citizenship*. 141.
19. Kymlicka, *Multicultural Citizenship*. 141. Kymlicka quotes from Young's article "Polity and Group Difference: A Critique of the Ideal of Group Citizenship."
20. Kymlicka, *Multicultural Citizenship*. 141.
21. Kymlicka, *Multicultural Citizenship*. 142.
22. Kymlicka, *Multicultural Citizenship*. 15.
23. Kymlicka, *Multicultural Citizenship*. 75.
24. Kymlicka, *Multicultural Citizenship*. 83.
25. Gerald Doppelt, "Is There a Multicultural Liberalism?" *Inquiry,* 41, (1998): 233.

26. Gerald Doppelt, "Illiberal Cultures and Group Rights," *Journal of Contemporary Legal Issues* 12 (2002): 671.

27. Kymlicka, "Reply." 79.

28. Kymlicka, "Reply." 79.

29. Kymlicka, "Reply." 72.

30. Charles Mills, *Blackness Visible: Essays on Philosophy and Race* (Ithaca: Cornell University Press, 1998).

31. Charles Mills, *The Racial Contract* (Ithaca: Cornell University Press, 1997): 56.

32. Mills, *Blackness Visible*. 134.

33. Mills, *Blackness Visible*. 105.

34. Mills, *Blackness Visible*. 113.

35. Mills, *Blackness Visible*. 78-81. These are obviously not strict conceptual categories, but rather, somewhat facetious descriptions of the flexibility of membership in "whiteness" conceived as a social category rather than a stable biological or phenotypic category.

36. Mills, *Blackness Visible*. 131.

37. Kymlicka, *Multicultural Citizenship*. 28.

38. Kymlicka, *Multicultural Citizenship*. 29-30.

39. Kymlicka, *Multicultural Citizenship*. 16.

40. Paul Sheehy, *The Reality of Social Groups* (Burlington: Ashgate Publishing, 2006): 78.

41. In *Wisconsin v. Mitchell* 508 U.S. 476 (1993), for example, the U.S. Supreme Court upheld the imposition of harsher penalties for crimes based upon prejudice due to the "greater individual and *societal* harm inflicted by bias-inspired conduct" (my emphasis). In specifying societal harm, the decision notes that "bias-motivated harms are more likely to provoke retaliatory crimes, inflict distinct emotional harms on their victims, and incite community unrest." Thus hate crimes harm not just individuals, but society at large as well, and especially members of the social groups that are targeted, justifying, in the court's opinion, harsher penalties.

42. Marilyn Frye, "Oppression," in *The Politics of Reality: Essays in Feminist Theory* (New York: Crossing Press, 1983): 8.

43. Frye, "Oppression." 11.

44. That is not to say, of course, that such categories actually are natural, or even that they must be thought to be so in order for the group to be considered oppressed. I only mean to point out that, as a matter of fact, the group categories that pick out oppressed groups often *are* considered natural in some unspecified sense. The view that gender groups are natural kinds is perhaps an even clearer example. See Frye, "Oppression." 7.

45. Ann Cudd, *Analyzing Oppression* (Oxford: Oxford University Press, 2006).

46. Cudd, *Analyzing Oppression*. 41.

47. For an interesting discussion of this question, see Charles Mills's "'But What Are You *Really*?' The Metaphysics of Race," in Mills, *Blackness Visible*. 41-66.

48. Mills, *Blackness Visible*. 84.

49. In fact, eye color, hair color, and other arbitrary physical characteristics have been used for the purpose of racial classification, as in the example of the so-called Aryan race. In this case then, nonvoluntary characteristics become socially relevant and provide the basis for social constraints.

50. One could take issue with these claims, insofar as the categorizations are not equal across the relevant divisions. Whiteness or maleness is usually not taken to define a person in the same way as blackness or femaleness often is. Rather, whiteness and maleness are generally considered coextensive with personhood generally, and so as the norm, while blackness and femaleness are, when considered at all, considered as special cases. Nonetheless, I think there is a more fundamental reason why the claim that oppressor groups are oppressed is wrong, and so I will leave this criticism aside and grant at least the initial premise that oppressor and oppressed groups are equally nonvoluntary.

51. Frye, "Oppression." 13.

52. Sally Haslanger, "Oppressions: Racial and Other," in *Racism in Mind*. edited by Michael P. Levine and Tamas Pataki (Ithaca: Cornell University Press, 2004): 97-123.

53. Haslanger, "Oppressions." 98.

54. Jorge Garcia is perhaps the staunchest defender of such a view, at least in relation to race, though he mostly refrains from using the term oppression to describe racism. See "The Heart of Racism." *Journal of Social Philosophy* 27 (1996): 5-45.
55. Haslanger, "Oppressions." 100.
56. Haslanger, "Oppressions." 102.
57. Iris Marion Young, *Justice and the Politics of Difference* (Princeton: Princeton University Press, 1990).
58. Carol Gould, *Globalizing Democracy and Human Rights* (Cambridge: Cambridge University Press, 2004): 111.
59. Gould, *Globalizing Democracy.* 110.
60. Gould, *Globalizing Democracy.* 109.
61. Gould, *Globalizing Democracy.* 110.
62. Ultimately, I think that this claim rests on at least two questionable assumptions. First, Gould seems to assume that racial identity itself cannot be understood in the more fluid and self-ascriptive sense that she reserves for cultural identity. Though she does point to "the affirmation of blackness in previous decades" as an example of an attempt to reappropriate, resignify, or self-ascribe a previously ascriptive racial identity, she claims, for reasons that are not made explicit, that this movement was still "defined reactively" in terms of earlier racist ascriptions. Further, she seems not to appreciate the extent to which the black nationalist movement she invokes only in this brief gesture developed *in opposition* to attempts to understand racial identity in terms of culture or ethnicity. This debate, which continues today, can be traced back at least as far as abolitionism, and the question of assimilation vs. emigration that it raised. (For example, see F. Douglass's "The Folly of Colonization," in *African American Social and Political Thought 1850-1920*. edited by H. Brotz (Transaction Publishers, 1992), on assimilation; and M. Delaney's *The Condition, Elevation, Emigration, and Destiny of the Colored People of the United States*. (Ayer Company, 1988), on emigration. A central question in this debate is whether "race pride" is a progressive or regressive strategy for emancipation and liberation more generally.) My point here is only that the question of whether racial identities could persist in a just, nonracist and truly democratic society is an open one, and that Gould seems to preclude this possibility prematurely, and without much justification.
63. Gould, *Globalizing Democracy.* 110, 123.
64. Gould, *Globalizing Democracy.* 126.
65. Gould, *Globalizing Democracy.* 125.
66. Gould, *Globalizing Democracy.* 123.
67. A significant exception to this claim is the presumed right to survival in general. A culture may cease to exist through time without necessarily being oppressed. On this issue, I am tempted to agree with Sheehy (*Reality of Social Groups*), who argues that "a group has no more right to everlasting survival (immortality) than an individual. Death may be an individual misfortune, but we have no right against it in itself, but against those who would expedite it by imposing their will upon us . . . for a group, its foreseeable demise is not enough to ground a right unless that demise results from the intention to willfully drive it from existence," 185. In the latter case, I suspect the harm intended toward the group can be understood in terms of oppression. But since cultural groups are not my concern here, I am comfortable to leave the issue without further argumentation.
68. Michael Walzer, "On Involuntary Association," in *Freedom of Association*. edited by Amy Gutmann (Princeton: Princeton University Press, 1998): 64.
69. Walzer, "On Involuntary Association." 64.
70. Walzer, "On Involuntary Association." 66.
71. One may think of examples that contradict this claim. Slavery is a good example of a completely involuntary association, but a slave can still escape, even if such an exit is treacherous and difficult. Yet this "break" is incomplete, insofar as an escaped slave was, for a long time, still considered a slave. It is only when the institution itself is altered (if not abolished) that the break is complete. In relation to identities rather than associations the impossibility is stronger still. A person considered black, or female, could undergo a sex change, skin bleaching, plastic surgery, and so on to try to shed his or her ascribed identity. Yet I would argue that, if all the facts about such persons were widely known, the majority of persons would still

conclude that such a person was "really" black or "really" a woman, drawing from the hegemonic classifications that their societies impose upon individual identities. Again, it is only when these hegemonic views are altered (or abolished) that a real break becomes possible. This latter task is precisely what I am attempting in these and the subsequent pages.

72. Walzer cites Kristeva's *Nations without Nationalism*. translated by Leon Roudiez (New York: Columbia University Press, 1993); and Kateb's "Notes on Pluralism." *Social Research* 61, no. 2 (1994).

73. Kymlicka, *Multiculturalism*. 141.

Chapter Two

Collective Identity, Group Rights, and the Liberal Tradition of Law

In the previous chapter, I introduced the claim that a fundamental right possessed by groups is the right not to be oppressed or (formulated positively) the right to self-ascription. This claim stands in need of further argumentation. In this chapter, I will argue that such a right is not only equal in importance to rights as they attach to individuals: I will argue further, that it is actually *foundational* for traditionally-conceived individual rights, and so in some sense prior to them. A proper understanding of the discursive justification of individual rights, I argue, vindicates this claim. Since I have developed this argument in opposition to liberal theories of multiculturalism, and drawing from Jürgen Habermas's discourse theory, I will use Habermas's own commentary on Charles Taylor's version of multicultural liberalism as a starting point for investigation.[1]

In that commentary, Habermas raises the question central to this chapter: "Can a theory of rights that is so individualistically constructed deal adequately with struggles for recognition in which it is the assertion of collective identities that seems to be at stake?"[2] Fairly straightforwardly, he answers in the affirmative. He argues that the recognition of cultural minorities "does not require an alternative model that would correct the individualistic design of the system of rights through other normative perspectives."[3] So, it would appear in the first place that Habermas would not agree with me about the shortcomings of a liberal individualist model, nor about the incommensurability of theories of cultural minority and theories of oppression. In fact, his commentary on Taylor amounts to a defense of a certain kind of liberalism, and relies on a distinction between "ethnic and cultural minorities" and "nationalist movements" that is virtually identical to Kymlicka's problematic distinction between ethnic groups and national minorities.[4] Still, Habermas's particular brand of liberalism is distinct from the theories of cultural minority that I have criticized; so much so, in fact, that I will argue that it can provide a crucial pillar in the normative foundation of a theory of oppression. This is because his apparent defense of liberal individualism can only be understood if one first grasps his critique of "subject-centered philosophy," and the "intersubjectivity" that replaces it and grounds the entirety of his philosophical project. It is in this intersubjective mode of analysis (that is, in *groups* of a special sort) that individual rights find their ultimate justification. I take this to be Habermas's unique philosophical contribution, which, again, is vastly different from the traditional liberal justification of rights, group or individual. In what follows, I will attempt to bring out this underlying theme and show how it goes a long way (though unfortunately not all the way) toward a justification of what I have identified as a fundamental group right: the right to self-ascription.

INTERSUBJECTIVITY AND THE INTERNAL RELATION BETWEEN DEMOCRACY AND THE RULE OF LAW

Habermas's dispute with Taylor's multiculturalism stems from his reading that "Taylor proceeds on the assumption that the protection of collective identities comes into competition with the right to individual (*subjektive*) liberties."[5] The former falls under Taylor's "politics of difference," while the latter falls under his "politics of equal dignity," both of which he thinks are equally necessary but often conflicting principles of modern liberalism. Yet Habermas finds this to be a false dichotomy. When properly understood, he thinks, individual rights and collective identities do not conflict, but form an "internal relation." That is, for Habermas, public and private autonomy are "equiprimordial."[6] As this thesis is central to Habermas's legal and political philosophy, and is perhaps the central focus of his recent work on law and human rights, it merits further consideration.

According to Habermas, modern political theory has never really reconciled its two fundamental influences. On the one hand, republicanism prioritizes the public autonomy of the citizen over the private autonomy of the individual. This view is supported by the insight that private liberties can only be exercised under the protection of a system of law. Going back at least to Aristotle, republicanism sees law as proceeding from a collective vision of the good life (i.e., it presupposes a shared *ethical* worldview, since citizenship is a kind of collective identity). On the other hand, liberalism prioritizes private autonomy and pre-political human rights. This view is supported by the insight that political will formation is only possible given the presumption of certain natural rights. These rights are understood as constraints on any system of law, rather than as a product of political will formation. Therefore one is a private individual first and a citizen second.[7]

These two traditions are often seen as conflicting, the former taking popular sovereignty as the foundation of modern democracy, and the latter taking human rights as the inalienable foundation of the modern constitutional state. Of course, the two are only opposed in concept, being actualized in the same structures of modern constitutional democracies. And for Habermas, the two forms of legitimation presuppose one another. This is because, as Kant recognized, law itself has a dual character. It must be considered simultaneously as a coercive mechanism limiting individual freedom and also as an expression of an autonomous will self-legislating.[8] That is, in spite of the fact that laws are coercive, they are legitimate only insofar as we can, at least in principle, consent to them. Thus legitimate laws are also "laws of freedom." Yet, unlike Kant, whose primary concern is the unchanging and eternal moral law, Habermas is concerned with positive law, which is historical and in principle revisable. "The idea of self-legislation by citizens," he says, "should not be reduced to the *moral* self-legislation of *individual* persons."[9] This is because Habermas means to reconstruct an alternative justification for a system of rights, one that is freestanding in relation to the justification of morality generally, and one that is not dependent upon a "monological" metaphysics of the individual.

According to Habermas, the trenchant difficulties involved in synthesizing the liberal priority of private autonomy and the republican priority of public autonomy stem from "certain premises rooted in the philosophy of consciousness" as well as "a metaphysical legacy inherited from natural law, namely, the subordination of positive law to natural or moral law."[10] The two phenomena are related, insofar as both rely on a traditional metaphysics of the subject, one which Habermas challenges in a unique way. For liberalism, the fundamentality of individual rights is normatively justified by reference to either natural law or a "metaphysics of morals." For Hobbes and Locke, for example, the fundamental rights of the private individual are justified by reference to certain laws of nature that are considered innate. Having such rights is simply part of what it means to be a rational human being, and is thus thought to require no further justification. What these theorists are more concerned with is the genesis of political authority and public rights. Such rights are justified only in a second step: the creation, through collective agreement, of an external sovereign to protect the private rights of individuals. Political sovereignty, then, and the set of political rights that citizens retain (which vary greatly from Hobbes to Locke), are only instrumentally valuable, and only legitimate insofar as they are derived from the pre-political rights of private individuals.

Whether or not this is a convincing account of the justification of political authority, it does not provide a very sophisticated account of the justification of private "natural" rights, especially when the natural law account is uncoupled from its metaphysical and religious foundations. Kant aimed to provide a deeper justification for these fundamental private rights in relation to morality rather than prudential rationality. The inviolability of individual persons expressed in private rights derives its legitimacy from a priori principles of practical reason demonstrable through a principle of universalizability: the categorical imperative. As moral beings, humans have the unique capacity to represent their will as objective law; that is, to express their autonomy in and through willing. The principle that binds the human will also proceeds from it. This makes practical reasoning a reflexive process, and it makes of each person an end in him or herself. The categorical imperative is the fundamental principle that expresses respect for persons as ends in themselves. In terms of right, it amounts to "the freedom of each to the condition of its harmony with the freedom of everyone."[11] The social contract, then, or "public right" is the differentiation of this single right into a system of rights designed to protect this morally necessary harmony. Yet these latter rights, though derived from the moral law, and so still a priori, are nonetheless "external" to it insofar as the moral law itself does not depend upon them for its legitimacy. So, although Kant imports rational (cognitive) moral content into the concept of public autonomy (unlike Hobbes or Locke), he still sees public autonomy as subordinate to private autonomy.

Habermas finds this problematic, in the first place because he finds the individualism of these explanations untenable. "At a conceptual level," he argues, "rights do not immediately refer to atomistic and estranged individuals who are possessively set against one another."[12] For liberals like Hobbes and Locke, whose social contractors have only self-interested reasons to enter into civil society, the rights bestowed upon them by this arrangement are only instrumentally justified. That is, in Kantian terms, their obligations to the law are only hypothetical, and not unconditional. Yet for Kant, the "monological" design of the Categorical Imperative fails to capture this very insight. For Hobbesian liberals, the parties to a social contract "would have to be capable of understanding what a social relationship based upon the principle of reciprocity even means."[13] But as pre-political individuals, they would only understand their freedom as a "natural freedom that occasionally encounters factual resistance," but not as a "freedom constituted through mutual recognition."[14] And though Kant recognizes this, and so attempts to give the social contract a more substantive moral foundation in rational autonomy, this foundation turns out to be incompatible with modern pluralist societies, which require "postmetaphysical" justifications of law and morality. Let me now explain this point in more detail.

As I have said, Kant's conception of morality, and thus, in turn, of private and public right, is founded upon the idea of freedom as autonomy. The free will that his moral theory requires is of a different sort than the simple freedom of choice that most liberal theories of right aim to protect (as is expressed in the German terms *Wille* and *Wilkur*). A central focus of Kant's critical project, then, is to reconcile freedom of the will with deterministic laws of nature, both of which he sees as equally necessary. This complex project leads Kant to posit a two-tiered metaphysics. In the *phenomenal* realm of appearances, the behavior of objects is governed by deterministic natural laws. This is the world of objects as we experience them. However, Kant finds it necessary to posit, in addition, the *noumenal* realm of "things in themselves," which must be considered exempt from these laws. However, "even with the closest attention and the greatest clarity that the understanding can bring to such representations, we can attain to a mere knowledge of appearances but never to knowledge of things in themselves."[15] This cognitive gap applies not only to objects outside of the subject, but, perhaps more importantly, to the subject itself. Kant asserts that an individual "must necessarily assume that beyond his own subject's constitution as composed of nothing but appearances there must be something else as basis, namely, his ego as constituted in itself."[16] Of this "transcendental ego," however, we can have no further knowledge. In particular, the freedom that grounds the moral law here becomes speculative, since free will must be a property of the transcendental ego. Free will, then, becomes a "postulate of pure practical reason," an axiomatic moral belief that cannot itself be theoretically justified.[17]

Habermas sometimes refers to this as the "doubling of the relation to self," and understands it as the result of "the objectifying attitude in which the knowing subject regards itself as it would entities in the external world."[18] This "philosophy of the subject" (or sometimes "philosophy of consciousness"), of which Kant is the prime example, is inadequate as a moral and legal foundation. Since the relation of the empirical (phenomenal) self to the transcendental (noumenal) self amounts, in the end, to a leap of metaphysical faith, morality must find a new justification *within* phenomenal reality; that is, within the "lifeworld" of empirical subjects. This justification cannot be based upon the individual subject, as is Kant's Categorical Imperative. It cannot assume that "each individual can project himself sufficiently into the situation of everyone else *through his own imagination*."[19] Instead, this act of individual imagination must be replaced by an actual discursive process. "When the participants can no longer rely on a transcendental pre-understanding grounded in more or less homogenous conditions of life and interests," he claims, "the moral point of view can only be realized under conditions of communication that ensure that *everyone* tests the acceptability of a norm."[20] The result is a principle of discourse, which is meant to apply not to individuals, but to groups of language users. In the concept of the lifeworld, the locus of intersubjective communication oriented toward mutual understanding, "*concrete* forms of life replace transcendental consciousness in its function of creating unity."[21] Understood as "intuitively present group solidarities," these concrete forms of life "only emerge in the plural."[22] Thus Habermas effectively replaces the monological reason of the philosophy of the subject with the *communicative* reason of a foundational intersubjectivity.

Why then, to return to the central question, would he *deny* that an individualistically constructed theory of rights is problematic, or that it requires an alternative normative justification, which is precisely what he affirms against Kantian morality? To answer this question, one must recall that Habermas resists the attempt to justify positive legal rights in moral terms. These public rights must be justified in their own terms, "in the medium of law itself."[23] So, one cannot assume that his criticisms of Kantian morality (including its monological individualism and its need of an alternative discursive normative foundation) apply automatically to individualistic justifications of law. However, Habermas does suggest that the principle of discourse he offers as an alternative to the Categorical Imperative can be "operationalized" for other types of discourse, including legal discourse.[24] The result is not a principle of morality, but a principle of *democracy*. The difference in the two principles derives from the difference in the types of norms that they purport to justify. Moral norms are universal in the strictest sense—that is, across space and time. They are the result of the *internalization* of the discourse principle by moral agents. That is, one acts morally when one acts according to reasons that everyone could accept. Such maxims cannot (and need not) in principle be legally regulated since they refer to internal motivations rather than external actions. Legal norms, on the other hand, govern the external relations of individuals insofar as they do or do not conform to certain rules of action. This is why legal norms take the specific historical form of individual rights, rather than the general abstract form of moral principles. The principle of democracy, then, is the result of the *institutionalization* of the discourse principle in the form of a system of rights. It assumes the private rights necessary for the creation of a political community, then it justifies those rights retroactively from the perspective of members of the political community themselves. This is what is meant by the co-originality of (or internal relation between) public and private autonomy, democracy, and the rule of law.

So, though legal norms are "individualistic" insofar as they must take the institutional form of individual rights, they are still justified discursively. The point is only that the discourse principle cannot be applied to moral and legal norms in a uniform way. The "legal person" is a necessary creation of a system of law that is nonetheless legitimated by reference to intersubjective processes of will formation. The fact that "the legal form has an atomizing effect," Habermas says, "does not negate the intersubjective bases of law as such."[25] That is, Habermas views the individuation of persons as a social process arising necessarily from established collective identities. This means that "every legal community and every democratic process is inevitably permeated by ethics."[26] However, the principle of democracy means to regulate this permeation, assuring that all ethical views receive fair hearing and that none unfairly bias the process of establishing basic rights. In short, though ethics may (and even should) permeate the democratic process, it does not determine it.

Now Habermas's subtle criticism of Taylor can be understood more clearly. By describing and then criticizing a view of the liberal state as ethically neutral, Habermas finds Taylor to be employing a straw-person fallacy. A system of rights that is individualistic *in form* can deal with struggles for the recognition of collective identities because it *must* deal with such identities in the first place, in order to be legitimate as a system of law. This is the very substance, Habermas thinks, of the democratic process. Furthermore, Habermas does not see his interpretation of liberal democracies as an alternative to traditional liberal and republican theories so much as a *reconstruction* of the *self-understanding* of liberal democracy. This is why ultimately, despite his fundamental critique of traditional individualism and the philosophy of the subject, and despite his reinterpretation of the basis of legitimation in terms of intersubjectivity, he denies the need for an "alternative model" based on "other normative perspectives." He thinks that liberal democracy itself implies his model of legitimation, and so it does not need to be supplemented or replaced, so much as properly understood. In light of this explication, let me now return to the issue of groups and group identity in order, ultimately, to show how the fundamental right of groups fits with Habermas's discursive account of legal rights.

COLLECTIVE IDENTITY AND POLITICAL INTEGRATION

As the above analysis begins to show, groups are essential to Habermas's discourse theory, despite his complex defense of a system of law that is "individualistic" in form. One could even go so far as to say that this is the main difference between his reconstruction of liberalism and classical liberalism. The latter, he thinks, fails to take into account the "forms of solidarity that link not only relatives, friends and neighbors within private spheres of life, but also unite citizens as members of a political community *beyond merely legal relations.*"[27] These two forms of solidarity are linked but nonetheless distinct. They form two levels of integration, corresponding to two levels of collective identification, which must not be conflated.

"Ethical-cultural" identity is a strong collective identity involving shared beliefs, traditions and practices. As such, it has much in common with Rawls's idea of a "comprehensive doctrine," as well as the idea of culture that informs the work of multicultural liberals like Kymlicka and Taylor. The difference, however, is that these groups are not mere aggregations of individual choices about the good life, but foundational intersubjectivities in which "persons are so to speak nodal points in an ascriptive network of cultures and traditions."[28] That is, this strong collective identity is the soil from which individuation and personal identity grow.[29] This makes groups prior to individuals, both conceptually and actually, at the level of ethical life. But Habermas carefully distinguishes ethics and ethical life from both morality and legality. While morality and legality employ discourses of *justification* aimed at demonstrating the validity of their respective norms, ethical discourses are discourses of *self-clarification* in which members of the group come to an agreement about their particular values and their ethical-political self-understanding. In modern pluralist societies this strong form of collective identity cannot form the basis of citizenship, since these societies contain diverse groups with fundamentally different values.

However, unlike Rawls, whose political liberalism sees the state as the neutral location for an overlapping consensus of worldviews, Habermas does see political membership as requiring a certain kind of shared collective identity, though much weaker than the identity shared by members of ethical-cultural groups.[30] The collective identity that constitutes citizenship "is rooted in an interpretation of constitutional principles from the perspective of the nation's historical experience."[31] Habermas thus sometimes refers to this kind of collective identity as "weak constitutional patriotism," but also as "ethical-political" identity. As a discourse on citizenship, it establishes the parameters within which the legal norms and the system of basic rights established by the constitution apply. This weak collective identity can integrate ethical-cultural groups without demanding that they assimilate to a particular value system or form of life (that is, a strong collective identity). In other words, all that can be demanded of members of the political community is "assent to the principles of the constitution."[32] Yet even this assent is interpreted from, and so rooted in, the perspective of particular ethical-cultural identities. That is, though political membership does not require allegiance to any *particular* ethical-cultural identity, it does ultimately derive its legitimacy from ethical-cultural identities in general. This is why Habermas asserts that "solidarity is the reverse side of justice."[33]

Oppression stands as a serious impediment to this type of political integration, and to the creation of a weak national solidarity, for a variety of reasons. This is most obvious when oppression takes the form of outright exclusion from the polity, as it often has in the past and sometimes still does today. However, oppression can impede political integration in more subtle ways, perhaps more common in contemporary liberal democracies. Insofar as oppression results in material inequalities, it may de facto preclude the possibility of the political participation of oppressed groups, even though such participation is supposedly protected in principle. This is the force of the Marxist criticism that liberal rights are merely formal rights and fail to secure the material bases necessary for enjoyment of those rights. Additionally, oppression destroys the trust and mutual respect necessary for the type of solidarity Habermas outlines. One might call this the *affective* basis of solidarity, distinct from its material bases, which have received greater theoretical attention. This suggests that, even if the formal and material bases of political integration are in place, such integration fails in the face of both "official disrespect" from the legal apparatus and lack of mutual respect among the ethical-cultural groups that would seek to form a minimal alliance for the purposes of democratic will formation.[34] Of course, in most cases of oppression, these forms overlap and coexist. Still, it makes some sense to make these analytic distinctions (which are, it will become clear, forms of group harm) in order to compare Habermas's thoughts on oppression with the definition of oppression provided in the first chapter.

Habermas takes oppression seriously as a failure of political integration, so much so that he states categorically that "in a legal community, *no one* is free as long as the freedom of one person must be purchased with another's oppression."[35] However, he does not ultimately see oppression as a fatal flaw in the system of rights he describes. By making rights subject to reinterpretation and revision according to a principle of democracy, Habermas thinks that the ideals of freedom and equality (which in principle rule out oppression) can be progressively realized. Habermas consistently uses feminism and the "feminist politics of equality" to illustrate this point. The oppression of women as a group has changed shape throughout history. Until relatively recently, this oppression took the most obvious form of outright exclusion from the polity. It was only within the past century that the *formal* equality of women was recognized in law, through the extension of voting rights. However, Habermas correctly notes that "the formal equality that was partially achieved merely made more obvious the ways in which women were *in fact* treated unequally."[36] In part to address this problem, the liberal paradigm of law, with its focus on formal equality, gave way to a social-welfare paradigm focusing on *material* equality. This paradigm urged not only formal equality, but also legal recognition of relevant *differences* between men and women. So, for example, the legal recognition of the fact that women (and not men) bear children led to the implementation of special protections and leaves of absence for pregnant women.[37] Such measures aim to ensure the effectiveness of equal basic rights by ensuring their material bases. However, as feminists like Nancy Fraser have pointed out, these measures of the social-welfare state have tended to further stereotypes of women as dependent, replacing the private paternalism of the husband with the public paternalism of the State.[38] In other words, though these measures aim to ensure the formal and material bases of inclusion, they fail to secure the affective basis of inclusion, instead showing women a kind of official disrespect that prevents them from being full autonomous members of the polis.

Habermas understands these two paradigms of law—liberal formalism and social-welfare materialism—as two poles of a "dialectic of legal and factual equality." A strict focus on formal legal equality—the right to vote, for example—aims to secure public autonomy at the expense of private autonomy. It legally mandates equal rights while ignoring the private barriers to exercising such rights: employment, education, health, wealth, and so forth. On the other hand, a strict focus on material equality—through social-welfare programs, for example—aims to secure private autonomy at the expense of public autonomy. In aiming to secure the material bases for the effective exercise of formal rights, the social-welfare state transforms the active, participatory citizen role into a passive, consuming client role. It thus disempowers the very groups it means to enable. Drawing from his thesis on the co-originality of public and private autonomy, then, Habermas introduces a third, *proceduralist* paradigm of law. According to this paradigm, the process of actualizing rights is discursive, based upon the self-interpretation of the groups to which laws and social programs are meant to apply. So, in the case of women, for example, neither a formal equality that ignores difference nor a social-welfare policy that reifies it will suffice. Instead, the relevant aspects of equality and difference (in short, the meaning of equal treatment) must be determined on a case by case basis by way of the deliberation of *the affected parties themselves*.[39] Here discourses of self-clarification take on a political character. Only through the self-interpretation of needs and the self-clarification of what it means to be (in this case) a woman can the relevant rights be actualized. This is the substance of a kind of "identity politics" that Habermas sees as crucial for the legitimation of a democratic system of rights.[40] I will discuss this discursive conception of identity politics in more detail in the next chapter. For now I only mean to point out that Habermas's proceduralist program for the actualization of rights requires something like what I have described as the fundamental right of groups: the right to self-ascription.

In the first chapter, I defended a definition of oppression as the systematic attempt to eliminate self-ascription leading to group harm. I also argued that theories of cultural minority are ill-equipped to deal adequately with this phenomenon, since they fail to recognize the fundamentality of groups as well as the fundamentality of conflict in its relation to the formation of non-intentional groups. So far in this chapter, I have attempted to show that groups of a certain kind are fundamental to Habermas's account as well, in spite of his assertion that at its point of application, the legal system must be individualistic in form. And in light of his analysis of feminism, one can also see that self-ascription plays a central role in the legitimation of rights, though he does not speak of it, as I have, as a right in itself. It remains to be shown, then, in what sense the right to self-ascription is, in fact, a right, what kind of right it might be, and where (if anywhere) it fits in Habermas's elucidation of the system of rights. First, however, I would like to continue the present line of inquiry beyond Habermas's example of feminism, in order to see whether it applies to other kinds of oppressed groups, and, most importantly, whether a general theory of oppression (which Habermas never really provides except in terms of specific examples) can be extracted from it.

This extended analysis is necessary, since Habermas asserts that, compared with feminism, "the struggle of *oppressed ethnic and cultural minorities* for the recognition of their collective identities is a different matter."[41] Already one should note the phrase "oppressed ethnic and cultural minorities," which conflates, I have suggested, two very different frameworks for understanding group identity. This difference is made explicit in his contrast of women with other oppressed groups, and it lies in the relation between the groups' strong ethical-cultural identity and the weak ethical-political identity of the citizenry as a whole. "Women's cultural self-understanding is not given due recognition," he says, "any more than their contribution to the common culture."[42] So, "the political struggle for recognition begins as a struggle about the interpretation of gender-specific achievements and interests."[43] That is, it begins as a discourse of self-clarification. Yet, "insofar as it is successful, it changes the relationship between the sexes along with the collective identity of women, thereby affecting men's self-understanding as well."[44] Thus the feminist movement represents what David Ingram, following Jean-Francois Lyotard, calls a "syncretist transformative" identity politics.[45] Through its own internal transformation, it transforms other types of identity as well, creating a new mélange of collective identification identical to none of its component parts.

However, Habermas does not see the self-clarification of cultural and ethnic identity as similarly transformative. "From the point of view of members of the majority culture," he says, "the revised interpretation of the achievements and interests of others does not necessarily alter their own role in the same way that the interpretation of the relations between the sexes alters the role of men."[46] There is some truth to this claim. The oppression of women is unique for many reasons, and it should not be conflated with the oppression of other minority groups, not least because women are not, after all, a numerical minority. And it is also true that cultural groups can sometimes, under normal circumstances, pursue their own way of life in isolation from the "majority" culture. But oppression represents a *departure* from the normal circumstances of collective identity formation. Oppression, as I have argued, is precisely the *suppression* of the kind of self-ascription that can make cultures appear autonomous and self-enclosed. And insofar as oppression is relational, it cannot be overcome without transforming its constitutive relation between oppressor and oppressed groups. Racial oppression, for example, involves (if not derives from) unwarranted feelings of superiority on the part of the "majority" race, made concrete in a variety of measures that share in common the attempt to inscribe inferiority as a part of what it means to be a member of a "minority" race. In this case, then, the reconstruction of a positive collective identity for racial minorities must also transform the self-understanding of its oppressor group. Otherwise, the weak national solidarity required of a successful democratic order collapses under the weight of different factions that each see themselves as superior to the others.

In other words, though there are important differences between women and other social groups, Habermas fails to identify the common conditions under which any such group can be called *oppressed*. Habermas likewise fails to recognize the relational dimension of oppression as well as the transformational character of self-ascription. These failures can be attributed to adopting the problematic framework of "cultures" in order to address the problem of oppressed groups. This framework presupposes intentionality as a defining characteristic of group membership, and so it understands the task of political integration as a matter of integrating preestablished *worldviews*. But oppression involves not just the struggle for recognition of a preestablished collective identity, as Habermas seems to suggest. It is the struggle for the very conditions necessary to construct such a vision of collective identity. Sometimes, as in the example of class and, according to some, race,[47] the political goal is recognition of the fact that the collective identity ascribed to a certain group is illegitimate; that there is, in fact, no basis for identification except the shared experience of oppression. In such cases, the goal is not group autonomy but self-eradication through transformation of society as a whole. The concept of culture is equally ill-equipped to speak to these kinds of cases. In sum, though Habermas's discourse theory provides a sophisticated model of what I have called normative intentionalism—the idea that socially relevant group membership *ought to be* based upon voluntary association, even if it currently is not—it is not explanatorily sufficient to ground the practice of democracy in nations where oppressed groups exist. This is because oppressed groups do not necessarily share an "ethical-cultural" identity, even though they do share an *ascribed* collective identity. This latter type of identity cannot be understood in terms of a "discourse of self-clarification" or a consensus on a conception of the good. It must be understood in systematic terms. I will now turn to such an explication.

PATHOLOGIES IN THE ACTUALIZATION OF RIGHTS

Habermas is as aware as anyone of the systemic inequalities present in actually existing liberal democracies. More than most contemporary political theorists, in fact, Habermas understands and takes seriously these empirical failures. This sensitivity to the shortcomings of the liberal-democratic state may be attributable to the influence of the tradition of critical theory on Habermas's work. As a retrieval of Marxist theory in light of developments in postindustrial capitalist societies, the question of group (namely class) membership and the problem of the oppression of the working class were central problems for first-generation critical theory. Theorists like Max Horkheimer, Theodor Adorno, and Herbert Marcuse aimed to show how the so-called freedoms of liberal democracy actually mask a more fundamental social domination—a domination manifested, on the one hand, in a technocratic state bureaucracy that replaces democratic decision-making with expert knowledge; and, on the other, in a mass mediatized "culture industry" that precludes even informal public criticism and ensures consent to the given form of social organization.[48] Of course, for critical theorists, these new forms of domination grow from and supplement the old form of domination: class exploitation. The technocratic state and the culture industry are the latest means by which the capitalist mode of production reproduces itself at the respective political and cultural levels.

From a philosophical perspective, critical theorists linked these forms of domination to reason itself. By subsuming the particular under the universal, reason itself, they thought, implies the erasure of difference and a "leveling abstraction," and so sets the groundwork for domination. Following Max Weber, they saw modernity undergoing a process of "rationalization" in which the "cultural value spheres" of art, science, and morality are separated and linked to specific purposive-rational governing procedures. Here the Enlightenment project of bringing rationalization to all spheres of life takes on an ideological character. The emancipatory self-understanding of this project conceals the fact that increased rationalization does not, in fact, lead to increased human freedom, but to its opposite. The rationalization of key areas of social life would lead ultimately, they thought, to totalitarianism. This final verdict on reason, however, seems to preclude rational emancipatory critique, insofar as such critique is itself based in reason. So, according to some, this increasing suspicion about reason itself undermines the very aims of critical theory.

As a student of critical theory, Habermas recognizes the dangers of technocracy, mass media, and economic exploitation, but he aims to address them without undertaking an all-encompassing critique of reason. Rather, by identifying norms implicit in everyday communication, Habermas reconstructs a form of rationality oriented to reaching understanding. This *communicative* rationality stands in a dialectical relation to the instrumental rationality that leads to domination. In this way, Habermas sees himself escaping the "dialectic of Enlightenment" that leads to the pessimistic vision of inescapable domination, instead theorizing a new foundation for critical resistance. This brief gloss cannot do justice to the complexity of Habermas's reconstruction of rationality, undertaken mainly in the two-volume *Theory of Communicative Action*. I mention this project only to demonstrate that concerns about the potential for domination in contemporary capitalist societies are at the heart of Habermas's social theory, and, more importantly, to show how his bifurcated conception of reason is mirrored in the distinction between system and lifeworld, which is of central importance to his political theory.

If communicative rationality is the capability of linguistic beings to come to understand one another, communicative action is the realization of this capability in discourse. As such, the theory of communicative action provides the substantive philosophical basis of discourse theory, which is fundamentally a theory of argumentative procedure. The concept of the lifeworld circumscribes the environment within which this type of action is possible. It is "the intuitively present . . . familiar and transparent, and at the same time vast and incalculable web of presuppositions that have to be satisfied if an utterance is to be at all meaningful."[49] That is, it is necessarily a contextual *background* for mutual understanding. Only when communication fails do these presuppositions come to the fore. Habermas gives the example of a construction worker telling another younger construction worker to fetch beer for lunch.[50] The presuppositions here include factual matters (that beer is available for sale, that it is feasible to walk to the store, etc.), as well as normative concerns (that it is acceptable to drink on one's lunch, that the "low man on the totem pole" is responsible for this task, etc.). If these implicit assumptions are not present, or misunderstood, then they must be reconstructed explicitly, or else the communicative lifeworld breaks down, and communication fails internally.

The ideally functioning lifeworld represents a space within which interlocuters can reach understanding without coercion. As such, the analysis of society from the perspective, of the lifeworld makes possible a vision of society as guided by the collective volition of its members. However, Habermas warns against a "hermeneutic idealism" that understands society as a whole in these intentionalist terms. The lifeworld perspective, he thinks, must be supplemented by another perspective that theorizes the *limits* of communicative action, as well as its impediments. The *systems* perspective, then, takes into account precisely those tendencies that Weber and early critical theorists saw as all-encompassing. Modern social systems like the state and the economy do take on an instrumental logic of their own, which is separate in principle from the rationality of collective action. In the first place, this is simply because increasing social complexity makes direct intentional control of complex social systems impossible. Perhaps in small, primitive societies, social organization could be understood solely in intentional terms. But in societies like ours, Habermas thinks, we cannot exchange goods and services by way of coming to mutual agreement about the value of goods in each case. So, a market economy arises, governed by the principle of supply and demand (or, if one prefers, the "commodity form"), to "unburden" the lifeworld of this demand. Similarly, we cannot feasibly come to agreement about every law or policy that presents itself in the political arena. So a representative system arises to carry out this task, a system which has, as the earlier analysis shows, a form and logic of its own (the individualistic "legal form").

In themselves, Habermas does not find these systems problematic. They arise to meet the needs of lifeworlds overburdened by social complexity. However, the instrumental rationality they employ as means to human ends does suffer from the dangerous tendencies that early critical theory identified. The logic of the commodity form, for example, tends by its very nature to expand beyond its proper scope, since capitalism cannot reproduce itself except through constant growth. This expansion is both horizontal, seeking out new markets for goods and services, and vertical, commodifying areas of human life previously considered sacred, or at least not subject to principles of exchange. The relinquishing of political authority to professional politicians also tends to expand beyond its necessity, insofar as it begins to view *all* political decisions as expert matters, creating a "democratic deficit" that undermines its own legitimacy. These are examples of the "colonization of the lifeworld" by systemic imperatives. With the image of colonization, Habermas means to acknowledge the dangers of Weberian rationalization that previous critical theorists recognized while still maintaining a theoretical space for critical reflection and transformation of these very systems.

The purpose of this excursus into Habermas's sociological framework of system and lifeworld is to see whether it is adequate for understanding oppression in systematic terms. More precisely, insofar as oppression inhibits the collective formation of will and identity characteristic of the lifeworld, and insofar as oppression is *systemic* (in a way yet to be fully worked out), one might say that oppression could be fruitfully conceptualized as a colonization of the lifeworld. But oppression does not seem to be a system in the same way that the economy or the state is, though it does operate through and within these systems. In what sense, then, can oppression be thought of as a system?

In the first place, the claim that oppression is systemic means that it is not simply reducible to the intentions of any particular group. I have claimed that neither oppressed nor oppressor groups should be conceived in intentionalist terms. The case, I think, is clear enough for oppressed groups, which are classified and defined in ways that do not depend on the will or consent of their members. One may think, though, that insofar as *oppressor* groups benefit from oppression, and even perpetuate it, both actively and passively, such groups ought to be understood intentionally. That is, it is tempting to conceive of oppression as a conscious, collective project undertaken by oppressor groups. In Habermasian terms, then, oppression would be a form of communicative action located within the lifeworld of oppressor groups but aimed at destroying the communicative capacities of targeted groups. Indeed, in talking about oppression under the rubric of "movements whose collective political goals are defined primarily in cultural terms," Habermas seems to lend credibility to this interpretation, and the standard of comparison among oppressed groups becomes the extent to which their own intentionally constructed self-understanding does or does not transform the self-understanding of other groups, or of society as a whole, understood here in terms of a communicative lifeworld.[51]

This intentionalist or "lifeworld" understanding of oppression contains some truth, but it misses crucial features of oppression. In many cases, for example, it is useful for conceiving the *historical origins* of systems of oppression. Charles Mills's theory of the "racial contract," for example, sees racial oppression arising from an explicit historical agreement on the part of whites to subjugate nonwhites, as the reader will remember from the first chapter. Somewhat similarly, Habermas's early work *The Structural Transformation of the Public Sphere* shows how the market economy and the oppressive class system that it engenders have their roots in the universalization of the particular collective self-understanding of the bourgeois class, institutionalized according to a principle of publicity.[52] As opposed to "scientific" interpretations of historical materialism, then, Habermas shows how capitalism and its characteristic mode of legitimation come into being through collective, intentional action. Yet both of these theories admit (even emphasize) that this original intentionality gets institutionalized or "reified" in systems that no longer depend upon explicit intentional direction. Thus Mills distinguishes between "signatories" to the racial contract and its "beneficiaries," the former representing the active constructors of the system of racial oppression (its "framers," as it were), and the latter representing the largely passive recipients of a system of privilege.[53]

In short, it is necessary to distinguish between the (nonetheless important) project of a genealogical analysis of the origins of oppression, for which intentionalist analysis may suffice, and the project of identifying (and eliminating) oppression in its current form, for which intentionalist analysis is insufficient. Once oppression is institutionalized, it takes on a systemic form that does not depend upon consent or intentional guidance for its reproduction. Today, focusing primarily on the intentions and attitudes of groups and individuals runs the risk of leading to the mistaken but all too familiar conclusion that since (some assume) prejudicial attitudes are less prevalent now than in the past, racism, sexism, and other systems of oppression no longer present the same challenges as they did for past generations. Rather, even if tomorrow, by some miracle of revelation, every person were purged of all prejudice and truly saw all others as their equals, oppression would remain so long as the structures that advantage some groups over others remain in place. At best, such a revolution in personal attitudes could provide the *motivation* to dismantle these structures of oppression, but it would not mark the end of oppression itself.

Oppression as "colonization of the lifeworld" captures the initial intentionality of oppression as well as the semiautonomous character it takes on once reified into systems. Once collective, willful oppression is solidified in systems of law, "objective" economic imperatives, and so on, oppressor groups are "unburdened" of the physical and psychological requirements of oppressing. Whites, for example, can now enjoy all the privileges of whiteness while simultaneously professing a cheery attitude of liberal tolerance. They can enjoy higher wealth and wages without the moral turpitude associated with expropriation. And they can hold the highest offices and positions while resting assured that everyone else had "equal opportunity" (no "special treatment") to hold them as well. In this way, the white psyche is insulated from the potentially harmful effects of oppressing, and is thereby enabled to construct a positive *individual* identity, supposedly separate from its membership in the white race.[54] Moreover, as Rousseau noted, oppression is necessarily institutional, insofar as it can only exist within the established institutions of civil society, and not in the "state of nature" as Hobbes, Locke, and others surmised. This is because in the lawless state of nature, the physical strength and psychological resolve required to thoroughly dominate another human being goes beyond the capabilities of any one individual, or would, at any rate, require such an individual to "expose himself voluntarily to a much greater hardship than the one he wants to avoid."[55] So, one can say that oppression unburdens the white lifeworld in a physical as well as psychological sense. In Weberian terms, the brute force of slavery is differentiated into various "rational" systemic mechanisms.

As one can imagine, these systemic mechanisms look very different from the perspective of those they oppress. Here the system does not enable the construction of identity, but rather prevents such collective self-identification through colonization of the lifeworld. And insofar as this colonization inhibits collective action precisely in the sphere that has the greatest impetus to transform the system, it serves the goal (like all colonizations) of system reproduction.[56] In other words, the unburdening function of oppression and its colonization function are unequally distributed in ways that facilitate system reproduction. Thus, as phenomenological accounts of oppression are especially adept at showing, oppressed identities are often felt as limiting rather than enabling. Linda Alcoff points out how in certain contexts—classroom discussions of race, for example—one's race or gender undermines one's authority and makes fruitful conversation difficult. In such cases, "the available options of interaction seem closed down to two: combative resistance without hope of persuasion, or an attempt to return to the category of nonthreatening other. "Neither," she notes, "can yield a true relationship or dialogue."[57] Here, then, is an unambiguous example of the ways in which systems of oppression, manifested in a kind of visual registry, literally impede communication.

Unfortunately, Habermas's generalized analysis of the colonization of the lifeworld does not shed much light on the differential distribution of the benefits and burdens of systems. Still, it does make some sense to analyze systemic oppression in general as well as particular terms. That is, though in one sense oppression benefits oppressors at the expense of those they oppress, in another sense, systems of oppression colonize the lifeworld of *all* citizens, insofar as oppression inhibits the ability of the citizenry to exert democratic control over systems in general. A society divided by oppression cannot reflexively actualize a system of rights in the way that Habermas outlines. This is because the vehicle or "sluice" through which communicative action exerts its political will—the public sphere—requires that no participants are privileged over others, such that the agreements produced are motivated solely by the force of the better reasons, and not by coercion. Yet oppression is precisely a system of privilege and coercive power—a system, as I have demonstrated, that inhibits the very capability to achieve mutual understanding even at the level of "ethical-cultural" self-understanding. Habermas recognizes this obstacle, but in his early attempts to understand democratic will formation in discursive terms, he aims to surmount it by claiming that social inequalities must be "bracketed" in public discourse, such that participants deliberate "as if" they were social equals. Nancy Fraser has convincingly criticized this presumption, doubting "whether it is possible even in principle for interlocuters to deliberate *as if* they were social peers in specially designated discursive arenas when these discursive arenas are situated in a larger societal context that is pervaded by structural relations of dominance and subordination."[58] It is unreasonable to think that the effects of these larger social structures—which discourage women and minorities from being outspoken, which provide unequal educational resources, which turn publicity in general into a commodity that only the most well-off can afford—can be simply neutralized for the purposes of public discourse. There is a significant difference between conceptually bracketing inequalities in order to demonstrate the *possibility* of reaching mutual understanding, as Habermas does in elucidating his discourse theory in general, and actually bracketing inequalities to effectively achieve such understanding. While the former is an impressive philosophical feat, the latter is a futile act of political imagination.

Rather, as Fraser rightly concludes, the discursive interpretation and justification of rights in a political public sphere (that is, democratic legitimation itself) requires *actual* substantive equality. And substantive equality in turn requires (in fact, entails) freedom from oppression. Habermas himself has come to accept this criticism. In *Between Facts and Norms* he notes, in an unusually provocative tone, that "only in an egalitarian public of citizens that has emerged from the confines of class and thrown off the millennia-old shackles of social stratification and exploitation can the potential of an unleashed cultural pluralism fully develop."[59] Yet beyond acknowledging it, Habermas seems not to take the criticism to require any significant revisions to his procedural account of legitimation. That is, he doesn't seem to appreciate the extent to which oppression corrupts and renders impotent the very discursive procedures he takes to be central to democratic will formation. Insofar as such will formation takes place through actual public discourse, and insofar as oppression inhibits this type of discourse in the very sphere that Habermas places at the crucial intersection of the formal state apparatus and the informal associations of civil society, oppression introduces an aporia into Habermas's reflexive mode of justification. Individual legal rights cannot be actualized because the forum in which they receive their legitimation becomes "desiccated." But this desiccated public sphere itself cannot be "repoliticized" without the participation-securing force of individual legal rights. In short, if democracy and legal rights are internally related in the way Habermas describes, then crises of democratic participation necessarily lead to crises in the justification of rights, and vice versa. In spite of his scattered condemnations of oppression, Habermas seems not to appreciate the seriousness of oppression as a crisis of just this sort, and so he fails to address it systematically. Some have suggested that this may be a principled oversight, since as a committed proceduralist, Habermas cannot justify strong condemnations of oppression with recourse to a substantive conception of justice.[60] But even if democracy and individual rights could be uncoupled, individual rights would be inadequate to prevent oppression, for all the reasons presented in the first chapter. Instead, I have suggested that *groups* must be understood as possessing a right not to be oppressed or, formulated positively, a right to self-ascription. Let me now turn, finally, to the specification of this right.

THE RIGHT TO SELF-ASCRIPTION: ITS TYPE AND JUSTIFICATION

What does it mean to say that groups possess a right to self-ascription? What status does such a right have within a democratic system of law? Is it "internally related" to democracy in the same way that individual rights are? In the first place it would seem that group rights cannot be legal rights, since Habermas insists that legal rights are, by definition, individualistic in form. Yet in more recent work, published after *Between Facts and Norms*, Habermas seems to take a softer stance on this matter, granting some weight to the idea of group rights. In his most recent examination of the politics of "multiculturalism," for example, he claims that "citizens in underprivileged conditions have the *right to compensation* when the opportunities and resources are missing for them to use their rights according to their own preferences and value-orientations."[61] This assertion admits of another level of rights, rights that apply when the "opportunities and resources" necessary to actualize individual rights (i.e., a functioning public sphere) are lacking. The type of compensation entailed by a "right to compensation" is not specified, though one can conclude from Habermas's critique of the social-welfare state that financial remuneration will not be sufficient to empower citizens as participants in the kind of discourses necessary for actualizing individual rights. At any rate, it does not immediately follow that such a right must be a group right. However, in explicating the kind of right he has in mind, he admits that the "incomplete inclusion" of oppressed groups "makes the introduction of collective rights understandable."[62] Further, he characterizes such collective rights as "rights to self-assertion," which aim to secure the conditions necessary for forming a stable collective (or "ethical-cultural") identity.[63] Such rights are necessary since it is only against the background of self-ascribed collective identities that group members can subsequently develop into individual persons and legal subjects.

Here Habermas conceives of something very close to what I have called the right to self-ascription. However, this right is prior and external to the individualistic legal order. Habermas explains:

> These relations of recognition, reaching beyond sub-cultural boundaries, can be promoted only indirectly—not directly—by means of politics and law. Cultural rights and a politics of recognition can strengthen the capacity for self-assertion by discriminated minorities, as well as their visibility in the

> public sphere, but the value-register of society as a whole cannot be changed with the threat of sanctions. The aim of multiculturalism—the mutual recognition of the equal status of all members—requires a transformation of interpersonal relations, which is produced via communicative action and ultimately gets into full swing only by way of debates over identity politics within the public sphere.[64]

In this passage Habermas attempts a sort of sleight of hand, admitting that the "relations of recognition" from which oppression departs are beyond the proper scope of legal regulations, but nonetheless implying that they can still be legitimated procedurally, by way of debates "within the public sphere." However, "the mutual recognition of the equal status of all members" cannot be both a goal and a precondition of a functional public sphere. In other words, if oppression contaminates the very procedures by which rights are legitimated, as Fraser, others, and I have argued, and as even Habermas seems to admit with his acknowledgment of compensation rights, then group rights aiming to "compensate" for the loss of procedural legitimacy cannot themselves be legitimated by reference to those same compromised procedures. That is, the right to self-ascription stands outside of the "internal relation" of democracy and individual rights.

So the question becomes, how can such a right be justified, if it is prior both conceptually and empirically to the individualist system of legal rights? What could it mean, for Habermas, to possess a right outside of the internal rights-democracy relation? Here it becomes necessary to distinguish between *legitimation*, which is the purely procedural means of obtaining legitimacy through consent, and *justification*, which requires substantive argumentation. The difficulty, of course, is that depending upon how strictly one understands Habermas's procedural and pragmatic orientation to political will formation, justification might for all practical purposes be reducible to legitimation. Then the substantive force of any given argument—what makes it justified— is simply that it is the result of a discursive procedure adhering to certain rules. Here one runs up against the limit of Habermas's discursive conception of rights. Since the right to self-ascription makes possible the very discursive procedures oriented to actualizing individual rights, it cannot itself be justified procedurally. Axel Honneth makes a similar point in saying that Habermas "cannot grant the demand for social equality conceptual priority over the principle of democratic will-formation; he has to make it dependent upon the contingent state of politically articulated goals."[65] However, the right to self-ascription, grounded as it is in the competency of groups to construct and interpret their collective identity, must be derived from a *substantive* commitment to the value of a certain kind of collective freedom. Habermas admits as much in saying that collective rights gain their efficacy primarily from communicative action and not from the purely procedural legitimating force of law. Therefore, the right to self-ascription cannot be understood as an individual legal right in Habermas's strict sense. It must rather be understood in a broader way, as having moral content, and perhaps even as a *human right*. Such a right is nonetheless presupposed by the conception of individual legal rights outlined above.

Honneth's recognition theory provides some further insight into how a right to self-ascription might be conceived. For Honneth, the normative force of rights derives from an underlying structure of recognition with moral content. Somewhat similarly to Habermas's conception of intersubjectivity (though influenced as much by Hegel as Kant), Honneth sees the mutual recognition characteristic of intersubjectivity as the precondition for the kind of autonomy that is presupposed by not only systems of law, but also conceptions of morality and of ethical life. In other words, Honneth sees mutual recognition as the foundation not only of law, but of social theory in general, including intimate relations and associational ties (or relations of "solidarity"). In the intimate sphere, relations of love (comprised of not only erotic, but also parental and filial love as well as friendship) make possible the development of *self-confidence*: the ability to recognize one's needs and desires as important. In the sphere of law, rights relationships provide each individual with the *self-respect* that accords to autonomous persons as self-legislating beings. This type of respect undergirds the legal equality necessary for the kind of collective, democratic will formation that Habermas describes. Beyond legal equality, however, persons must also develop a sense of *self-esteem*, deriving from the recognition of those particular talents and characteristics that make them unique, and so different from others. In the cultural sphere, then, relations of solidarity (which Honneth conceives in terms of voluntary association around shared interests) form the background against which such self-esteem can develop.[66]

These three relations to self—self-confidence, self-respect, and self-esteem—developed through the internalization of intersubjective relations to others, represent the foundation upon which personal identity is built. Without them, persons cannot develop into the autonomous individuals that modern social, political, legal, and moral theory most often assumes. This foundational intersubjectivity comes very close to Habermas's account of the intersubjective basis of discourse, as described above. Further, the account of a legal sphere of rights based upon formal equality separate from the "cultural" sphere of voluntary association mirrors Habermas's distinction between the individual subject of law and the "ethical-cultural" identity of persons. The crucial difference, however, is that while Habermas sees intersubjectivity as providing the *possibility* of producing normatively binding agreements through discourse, Honneth sees this intersubjectivity itself as normative, taking empirical "struggles for recognition" and the phenomenological experience of disrespect as evidence of this normativity. This results in the further difference that while Habermas subsequently develops specialized, independent discourses for each of the spheres of morality, law, and ethics, Honneth develops a comprehensive view of society as a scheme of social cooperation, in which legal rights play an important but not exhaustive part.

From this more general (but also, in a sense, more concrete) perspective, one can see that the procedural justification of rights (which is not incompatible with Honneth's account) is only a part, albeit a crucial one, of a functioning democratic society. Since the ability to engage in discourses in general depends upon not only the self-respect provided by legal equality, but also the self-confidence provided by intimate relations and the self-esteem provided by associational life, the latter two activities or aspects of the lifeworld must also be seen as foundational to political life, and so appropriately protected. If one thinks of such protections in terms of rights (perhaps in terms, again, of *human rights*) it makes some sense, as I will now argue, to speak of rights outside of the framework of legally enforceable claims, even though both Honneth and Habermas tend to speak of rights only in that highly specific sense. One particularly productive way of understanding rights in this extra or pre-juridical sense is in terms of *capabilities*, a notion that has received much theoretical attention in recent years, and shares a certain affinity with Honneth's recognition-based theory.

Drawing in certain ways from Marx as well as Aristotle, the capabilities approach to rights suggests that what it means to have a right is to be capable of using it effectively. Thus rights point to one or more underlying capabilities which are themselves derived from a minimalist notion of human flourishing: the basic conditions under which any human being has a chance of pursuing a worthwhile life, however he or she understands that. That is, whatever one's culture, identity, or "conception of the good," there are certain basic necessities, such as food, water, and shelter, as well as more truly human needs (those associated with what Marx called our "species being"), like the need to associate with others and, perhaps, the need to express creativity through productive labor, without which *any* human life must be considered impoverished. This minimally substantive notion of human flourishing must be seen, capabilities theorists argue, as preceding rights, political or otherwise, and its actualization must be seen as the object of those rights themselves.

Of course, such a justificatory strategy requires the difficult and controversial task of specifying which capabilities are, in fact, universally necessary for human flourishing, a task that Martha Nussbaum, for example, takes on directly by providing no less than a list of "central human functional capabilities."[67] My argument here is more modest. I would suggest, first, that even if one finds the project of listing the central human capabilities problematic, the capabilities approach to rights suggests that a procedural approach to justification by itself is inadequate. To quote Nussbaum, "on the general issue of political justification, it is plain that people's intuitions about how to proceed vary greatly: some think we only put things on a sound footing when we devise a procedure that generates the good as an output, and others (including I myself) tend to think that our intuitions about the central capabilities are at least as trustworthy as our intuitions about what constitutes a good procedure."[68] This means that rights, political and otherwise, have an *intrinsic* value, in addition to their instrumental value in relation to the task of political will formation.[69] My second specific suggestion, then, is that the right to self-ascription must also be seen as having an intrinsic value, in addition to its instrumental value in making possible individual rights of the type discussed above. It points, that is, to a model of *intersubjective* human flourishing: an ideal of associational life that is not exhausted in or reducible to the ideal of the flourishing individual. And though it is not necessary for my argument to fully describe such a model, let it suffice to say that its presuppositions (say, that human beings are language users, for one) would likely prove far less controversial than those that underlie an individualist model of human flourishing that depends upon the politically and ontologically loaded view of persons as rational, autonomous subjects.

Such substantive accounts of the justification of rights, Honneth's as much as Nussbaum's, understand human rights ultimately in moral terms. Yet they can avoid Habermas's objection to theories of legal right derived from morality if, *contra* Honneth, one recognizes that the sphere of legal relations is not exhausted by its respect-securing function. That is, though legal rights may be crucial for developing the self-respect necessary for moral agency, and though likewise persons may be said to have a moral claim to such legal recognition (a "right to have rights," as some put it), it *does not* follow that legal rights must be justified in moral terms. That persons have a moral right to legal recognition in general does not establish the legitimacy of any right or set of rights in particular. These rights must still be legitimated in their own terms, through the types of discourse that Habermas describes. One might say, then, that the morality of legal rights underdetermines their legitimacy as laws. Rather, moral, or human rights, like the right to self-ascription, and the structure of recognition from which they can be derived, stand in a "complementary" relation to legal rights, as Habermas recognizes.[70] This means, on the one hand, as I have tried to emphasize throughout this chapter, that procedures aimed at justifying legal rights must be supplemented by substantive moral principles in lifeworld contexts that "meet them halfway."[71] On the other hand, as has yet to be fully clarified, the complementary relation of legal and moral rights also means that the latter must be supplemented by legal protections in order to be rendered effective.

The crucial point, however, is that legal and moral rights are distinct, and that the former must not be seen as derivative of the latter. As theorists of human rights have often pointed out, it seems intuitively plausible that persons have certain rights even if those rights are not solidified in law, for example, in places where child labor, slavery, and other forms of exploitation are still legally practiced. Yet even where such abuses are prohibited in law (and assuming even that these prohibitions are well constructed and more or less effective), they fail to clarify the positive aspects implied by the moral right. In other words, purely negative legal prohibitions are not sufficient to ensure the development of self-confidence (for example) in the way Honneth prescribes. Rather, the development of the requisite self-confidence requires a specific kind of care that is better captured in the positive formulation, "the right to adequate care," and this positive element cannot be dictated by law. That is, the law cannot prescribe the meaning of "adequate care." It can only prohibit certain gross violations in a negative fashion, and perhaps uphold certain widely accepted positive elements, like public education and basic health care. This further testifies to the pre-legal (or perhaps extralegal) character of a robust notion of rights.

Likewise, the collective right to self-ascription stands outside the realm of law proper, since, as Habermas recognizes, "a legal obligation to be in solidarity would be a contradiction."[72] Further, though one might see legal devices like the right to free association, freedom of religion, nondiscrimination measures, and so on as complementary to the right to self-ascription, the link is much more complex in this case, due to the fact that these measures apply in the first place to individuals rather than groups.[73] A further problem with such measures is that in practice they have tended to take the existing demography of social groups as a given, aiming at best to provide individual group members with equal resources and equal representation, rather than securing the ability of groups to (re)construct their own collective identities. In other words, the link between the moral right of groups to self-identify and the complementary legal protections that aim to prohibit actions inimical to that right is strained by the fact that the primary barriers to self-ascription are not individual acts but systemic tendencies. Unlike individual crimes, which correspond readily to legal remedy in a formally individualistic system of law, the perpetrators of group harm are more difficult to pinpoint, making legal remedy by way of such a system problematic. Still, it is not unthinkable that a system of law that considered oppression more carefully could find a way to buttress the right to self-ascription through legal rights. Even if this were to happen, however, the right to self-ascription would be conceptually distinct from legal rights as such.

In short, just as legal rights are, under ideal circumstances, actualized in discursive processes of political will formation, the substantive right to self-ascription is actualized by way of "struggles for recognition" in which groups aim to reconstruct and reinterpret their collective identity; that is, by a so-called "identity politics." Insofar as the justification of rights requires social equality, it presupposes struggles of this kind, such that the right to self-ascription is a precondition for the individual rights reflexively justified in formal political discourses. In this regard, recognition theory and capabilities theory provide similarly appropriate supplements to Habermas's procedural theory of democracy and rights. The views are not mutually exclusive. In fact, they are complementary for understanding not only the legitimacy of democratic law in a general sense, but for understanding how such an ideal can be achieved given the current state of society and the existence of oppressed groups. Further, the vision of identity politics largely shared (at least) by Habermas and Honneth provides the key to understanding how the problem of oppression can be addressed democratically. Yet many worry that the turn toward identity and recognition in political theory sets a dangerous precedent, overlooking distributive injustices, fetishizing identity, or legitimizing "illiberal," intolerant, or undemocratic groups. In the next chapter, then, I will provide an account of identity politics that avoids such worries; one that is informed by the problem of oppression I have outlined, that avoids the pitfalls of multicultural liberalism I have identified, and that can fit within a more general theory of democracy like the one described above.

NOTES

1. Jürgen Habermas, "Struggles for Recognition in the Democratic Constitutional State" in Taylor. *Multiculturalism*. 107-48.
2. Habermas, "Struggles for Recognition." 107.
3. Habermas, "Struggles for Recognition." 113.
4. Habermas, "Struggles for Recognition." 117-18.
5. Habermas, "Struggles for Recognition." 110.
6. Habermas, "Struggles for Recognition." 113.
7. Jürgen Habermas, "Remarks on Legitimation through Human Rights," in *The Postnational Constellation: Political Essays*. translated by Max Pensky (Cambridge, MA: MIT Press, 2001): 116.
8. Jürgen Habermas, "On the Internal Relation between Democracy and Law," in *The Inclusion of the Other: Studies in Political Theory* translated by William Rehg, (Cambridge, MA: MIT Press, 1999): 255.
9. Jürgen Habermas, *Between Facts and Norms: Contributions to a Discourse Theory of Law and Democracy*. translated by William Rehg. (Cambridge, MA: MIT Press, 1999): 121. Original emphasis.
10. Habermas, *Between Facts and Norms*. 84.
11. Immanuel Kant, *Practical Philosophy*. translated by Mary Gregor (Cambridge: Cambridge University Press, 1996): 290.
12. Kant, *Practical Philosophy*. 88.
13. Kant, *Practical Philosophy*. 91.
14. Kant, *Practical Philosophy*. 91.
15. Immanuel Kant, *Grounding for the Metaphysics of Morals*. translated by James W. Ellington. 3rd ed. (Indianapolis: Hackett Publishing, 1993): 52.
16. Kant, *Grounding for the Metaphysics of Morals*. 53.
17. Kant, *Practical Philosophy*. 238.

18. Jürgen Habermas, "An Alternative Way Out of the Philosophy of the Subject: Communicative versus Subject Centered Reason," in *The Philosophical Discourse of Modernity: Twelve Lectures*. translated by Frederick Lawrence (Cambridge, MA: MIT Press, 1987): 298.
19. Jürgen Habermas, "A Genealogical Analysis of the Cognitive Content of Morality," pp. 3-46 in *The Inclusion of the Other*.
20. Habermas, "A Genealogical Analysis of the Cognitive Content of Morality." 33.
21. Habermas, "An Alternative Way Out of the Philosophy of the Subject." 326.
22. Habermas, "An Alternative Way Out of the Philosophy of the Subject." 326.
23. Habermas, *Between Facts and Norms*. 120.
24. Habermas, *Inclusion of the Other*. 46.
25. Habermas, *Inclusion of the Other*. 112.
26. Taylor, *Multiculturalism*. 126.
27. Jürgen Habermas, "Equal Treatment of Cultures and the Limits of Postmodern Liberalism." *The Journal of Political Philosophy* 13 no. 1 (2005): 1-28. My emphasis.
28. Habermas, *Inclusion of the Other*. 145.
29. On this point Habermas's view has more in common with the Hegelianism of Taylor than with the individualism of Rawls and Kymlicka, though the communicative basis of intersubjectivity differs from Hegelian recognition theory in important ways. See Charles Taylor, *Sources of the Self* (Cambridge, MA: Harvard University Press, 1992).
30. See "Political Liberalism: A Debate with John Rawls," pp. 49-105 in *Inclusion of the Other* as well as John Rawls's "Reply to Habermas," in *Political Liberalism* (New York: Columbia University Press, 1996): 372-435.
31. Taylor, *Multiculturalism*. 134.
32. Taylor, *Multiculturalism*. 138.
33. Habermas, *Inclusion of the Other*. 14.
34. This is one reason why both Habermas and Rawls agree that even a liberal democratic system of law has its limits, and cannot accommodate fundamentalist or illiberal groups that refuse to recognize the legitimacy of other worldviews. For further discussion of the grounds upon which a political body can legitimately exclude certain groups or factions, see chapter 3.
35. Habermas, *Between Facts and Norms*. 418.
36. Habermas, *Inclusion of the Other*. 263. Original emphasis.
37. The most significant of these are the Pregnancy Discrimination Act of 1978 (P.L. 95-555) and the Family and Medical Leave Act of 1993 (P.L. 103-3, 107 Stat. 6).
38. Nancy Fraser, "Struggle over Needs: Outline of a Socialist-Feminist Critical Theory of Late-Capitalist Political Culture," in *Unruly Practices: Power, Discourse, and Gender in Contemporary Social Theory* (Minneapolis: University of Minnesota Press, 1989): 109-42.
39. Habermas, *Between Facts and Norms*. 425.
40. Habermas, *Between Facts and Norms*. 426.
41. Taylor, *Multiculturalism*. 117.
42. Taylor, *Multiculturalism*. 117.
43. Taylor, *Multiculturalism*. 117.
44. Taylor, *Multiculturalism*. 117.
45. David Ingram, *Rights, Democracy, and Fulfillment in the Era of Identity Politics: Principled Compromises in a Compromised World* (Lanham, MD: Rowman Littlefield Publishing Group, 2004).
46. Taylor, *Multiculturalism*. 118.
47. See my discussion of racial eliminativism in chapter 4.
48. See Max Horkheimer and Theodor Adorno, *Dialectic of Enlightenment: Philosophical Fragments*. edited by Gunzelin Schmid Noerr, translated by Edmund Jephcott (Stanford: Stanford University Press, 2002); as well as Herbert Marcuse, *One Dimensional Man* (Boston: Beacon Press, 1991.)
49. Jürgen Habermas *The Theory of Communicative Action. Vol. 2. Lifeworld and System: A Critique of Functionalist Reason*. translated by Thomas McCarthy (Boston: Beacon Press, 1981): 131.
50. Habermas, *The Theory of Communicative Action. Vol. 2.* 121-22.
51. Taylor, *Multiculturalism*. 117.

52. Jürgen Habermas, *The Structural Transformation of the Public Sphere: An Inquiry into a Category of Bourgeois Society*. translated by Thomas Burger (Cambridge, MA: MIT Press, 1989).

53. Mills, *Racial Contract*. 11. Mills claims that "all whites are beneficiaries of the Contract, though some whites are not signatories to it." An important caveat is necessary here. I do not think Mills means to attach normative importance to this distinction, for example, by implying that it is less morally culpable to benefit from oppression than to will it. At any rate, my argument here does not imply any such normative dimension. For the moment, I am concerned only with demonstrating that intentionalist explanations *alone* are inadequate for fully understanding systems of oppression.

54. Mills understands this in terms of an "epistemology of ignorance," a willful, collective misunderstanding that provides for whites the "cognitive and moral economy psychically required for conquest, colonization, and enslavement." Mills. *Racial Contract*. 19. My point here is similar, though it is ambivalent about the stronger claim that this "unburdening" requires a special epistemological framework for its analysis.

55. Jean-Jacques Rousseau, *Basic Political Writings* (Indianapolis, IN: Hackett Publishing, 1987): 58-59.

56. This is perhaps the reason why Habermas is pessimistic about the transformational potential of "the new type of underprivilege" that has replaced, for the most part, overt class conflict. Habermas suggests that a "new conflict zone" capable of system transformation will more likely grow from the ranks of the *privileged*, which is why he was tentatively optimistic about the growing student movements of the late 1960s and 1970s. I think this claim is ultimately mistaken, but at any rate, it does demonstrate the seriously disabling character of colonization.

57. Linda Alcoff, "Toward a Phenomenology of Racial Embodiment," *Radical Philosophy* 95 (May/June 1998): 26.

58. Nancy Fraser, "Rethinking the Public Sphere: A Contribution to the Critique of Actually Existing Democracy," in *Habermas and the Public Sphere*. edited by Craig Calhoun (Cambridge, MA: MIT Press, 1992): 120.

59. Habermas, *Between Facts and Norms*. 308.

60. Simone Chambers, "Can Procedural Democracy Be Radical?," in *The Political*. edited by David Ingram (Malden, MA: Blackwell Publishers, 2002): 168-88; and William E. Scheuerman, "Between Radicalism and Resignation: Democratic Theory in Habermas' *Between Facts and Norms*," in *Habermas: A Critical Reader*. edited by Peter Dews (Oxford: Blackwell Publishers, 1999): 153-77, make similar points.

61. Habermas, "Equal Treatment of Cultures." 14. My emphasis.

62. Habermas, "Equal Treatment of Cultures." 18.

63. Habermas, "Equal Treatment of Cultures." 18.

64. Habermas, "Equal Treatment of Cultures." 15.

65. Axel Honneth, *Disrespect: The Normative Foundations of Critical Theory*. translated by Joseph Ganahl (Cambridge: Polity Press, 2007): 235.

66. Axel Honneth, *The Struggle for Recognition*. translated by Joel Anderson (Cambridge: Polity Press, 1995).

67. Martha Nussbaum, *Women and Human Development: The Capabilities Approach* (Cambridge: Cambridge University Press, 2000): 78.

68. Nussbaum. *Women and Human Development*. 150.

69. In the footnote corresponding to the sentence quoted above, Nussbaum criticizes Habermas on precisely this point, and claims that taking seriously the intrinsic value of rights requires "diverging in a major way from Habermasian proceduralism." I agree with her criticism, but I think she overstates the case somewhat, since Habermas's proceduralism is not *incommensurable* with the substantive arguments provided by her capabilities theory as well as Honneth's recognition theory. In other words, her criticism suggests that Habermas's procedural account of (political) rights is *incomplete*, rather than fundamentally flawed.

70. Habermas, *Between Facts and Norms*. 111-18.

71. Habermas, *Inclusion of the Other*. 252.

72. Habermas, "Equal Treatment of Cultures." 4.

73. Indeed, many, if not most, accounts of group rights focus on these types of rights, rights that *individuals* can enjoy only as members of groups. This differs, however, from rights that attach to groups qua groups. The right to self-ascription, I have argued, is a group right in the latter sense.

Chapter Three

Identity Politics within the Limits of Deliberative Democracy

In the first chapter of this book, I began with a critique of multicultural liberalism based upon its inability to adequately address the issue of oppression: the ways that oppression problematizes the group concepts that it employs as well as the theory of group rights that it develops. One of the main problems with this view is that it understands group membership in what I have called *intentional* terms. That is, it sees group membership as paradigmatically consisting of the aggregation of conscious, voluntary, individual choices about who one associates with and why. This model of group membership, I have argued, does not capture (and even obfuscates) the nature of membership in oppressed groups, which are based largely on external, nonvoluntary forces. Yet I distinguished a descriptive intentionalism of this sort from *normative* intentionalism, in order to capture the insight that groups ought to be able to self-ascribe their collective identity, even if they are currently prevented from doing so in oppressive societies like our own. In the second chapter, I developed the guiding idea of normative intentionalism in terms of a "right to self-ascription." I showed how that right could fit within a Habermasian theory of democracy appropriately supplemented by Honneth's morally infused notion of "struggles for recognition," as well as an "identity politics" that both see as crucial to the practice of democracy and the justification of rights. In this chapter, I will flesh out this notion of identity politics and defend it against the many objections that have been raised by that controversial notion. In particular, I will demonstrate that identity politics properly conceived does not uncritically fetishize identity, nor does it legitimize any and all collective identities. Rather, by understanding how collective identity is discursively constructed, and thus governed internally by certain rules of discourse, it becomes clear that identity politics can be seen as a normative enterprise crucial to a functioning democratic society, and not just as a politics of self-interest located at the level of groups rather than individuals.

Such an analysis must take care not to conflate its ideal and nonideal aspects, however. Just as one must distinguish between descriptive and normative intentionalism in order not to overlook oppressed groups, one must distinguish between what might be called *retributive* identity politics—identity politics undertaken by oppressed groups aimed at ending their oppression—and the kind of identity politics that would remain a crucial part of ideal democratic functioning even in non-oppressive societies. As Linda Alcoff nicely summarizes, "the desire to be free of oppressive stereotypes does not necessarily lead to the desire to be free of all identity."[1] The goal of shedding oppressive stereotypes, then, does not exhaust the scope of identity politics. Rather, insofar as collective identity provides the context within which even ideal democratic deliberation takes place (as I argued above), one must also theorize the role of collective identity in relation to the ideal of democracy itself. I will refer to this latter kind of identity politics as *discursive-democratic* identity politics, without meaning to imply that retributive identity politics is somehow undemocratic. Insofar as possible, then, my analysis of identity politics and its detractors will follow this analytic distinction. Ultimately, however, the link between the two forms must also be made clear, in order to demonstrate that identity politics is not a mere recreation of a politics of self-interest.

RETRIBUTIVE IDENTITY POLITICS

Identity politics, in some sense a recent phenomenon, nonetheless draws from and continues a tradition of collectivist thinking dating back at least as far as Marx. Indeed, Marx was perhaps the first to show how systems of oppression manifest themselves through the construction of ascriptive identities: lord and serf, freeman and slave, bourgeoisie and proletarian.[2] Under capitalism specifically, it was the proletariat as "universal class" that, through pursuing its own liberation, held the key to the liberation of society generally. Thus the Marxist program of proletarian revolution can be understood, to a certain extent, as a kind of identity politics. Of course, Marx's blindness to other sorts of conflicts and oppressions—patriarchy, white supremacy, anti-Semitism, and so on—was in part what cast shadows of doubt upon his theory of historical materialism. Yet despite these shortcomings, the allocation of a "world-historical" task to a particular social group was, in fact, historically new, and, important criticisms notwithstanding, provided a model for future identity politics focused on overcoming other forms of oppression.

In the wake of the fragmentation of the traditional working class as Marx conceived it, collective identity became a central concern for the Marx-inspired tradition of critical theory. Once increasing social complexity and unanticipated developments in the division of labor rendered doubtful Marx's predictions about proletarian revolution, critical theory faced the task of reconceptualizing class in a way that could make sense of these empirical developments, or else locating the potential for revolutionary transformation in another kind of collective identity. Such a task was part of the broadly interdisciplinary research program undertaken by the "Frankfurt School" Institute for Social Research. Habermas inherited this program, which he pursued primarily in the general philosophical terms of a reconceptualization of rationality capable of "structural transformation." However, Habermas's general theory of rationality was complemented by an empirical concern for locating "new conflict zones" capable of using "communicative rationality" for (revolutionary) transformative ends, especially in his early writings. In "Technology and Science as Ideology," for example, Habermas argues that despite the demise of a unified and clearly distinguishable working class, class distinctions persist in a "generalized interest in perpetuating the system . . . in a structure of privilege."[3] By "structure of privilege," Habermas means to point to the fact that, although the traditional class-based division of labor (between wage laborers and owners of capital) has given way to more complex divisions, a latent class structure remains, visible by the clear discrepancy among the life chances of different groups (for example, between the growing underclass of service industry workers and most other sectors of society). And in lieu of proletarian revolution, Habermas anticipates "a new conflict zone," which "can only emerge where advanced capitalist society has to immunize itself, by depoliticizing the masses . . . in the public sphere administered through mass media."[4]

Remembering that this essay was written in the politically turbulent year of 1968, when student activism throughout the world appeared to be gaining steam as a formidable social force, it is not particularly surprising that Habermas tentatively located the potential for such a "new conflict zone" within this privileged sector of society. Yet, it is surprising that Habermas virtually dismisses the equally turbulent struggles around race and racism that also marked the period. "Who will activate this conflict zone is hard to predict," Habermas admits, but "neither the old class antagonism nor the new type of underprivilege contains a protest potential whose origins make it tend toward the repoliticization of the desiccated public sphere."[5] Habermas does not explicitly identify racism and white supremacy in his discussion of the "structure of privilege," but the familiar racial inequalities in education, employment, and general life chances make it reasonable to include these forms of privilege within this structure, even though they are not particularly new. One, then, ought to ask: What do these struggles lack such that Habermas doubts their ability to repoliticize a "dessicated" public sphere? Why must this new zone of conflict emerge out of the ranks of the privileged? In response to this question, Habermas offers a few brief observations. First, student activists' "social origins do not promote a horizon of expectations determined by anticipated exigencies of the labor market."[6] Their critical perspective, in other words, is not primarily determined by the necessity of finding and keeping work. Accordingly, then, "students are not fighting for a larger share of social rewards in the prevalent categories: income and leisure time"; rather, "their protest is directed against the very category of reward itself." Habermas, following Marcuse (indeed, he dedicates this essay to him), assumes that transformation of existing structures of legitimation can only be undertaken by those who have transcended their necessity. The struggles of the underprivileged, similar in this respect to traditional labor struggles, "merely" desire full inclusion in the system that excludes them: full citizenship, better wages, and so on.

In hindsight, Habermas's optimism about the transformational potential of student protest may appear somewhat naive. Yet such necessarily vague speculation illustrates that Habermas did not underestimate the importance of actualizing a potentially revolutionary new form of rationality in real political movements, and that this "unfinished project of modernity" would not be undertaken by philosophers and politicians, but by the people themselves. Of course, "the people" can be a dangerous placeholder, and this early essay betrays a troubling tendency in critical and Marxist theory, tracing back at least to Leninism, to see the masses as too deceived, too disenfranchised, and too utterly dominated to successfully fight for their own liberation, such that that task must be undertaken by advocacy, be the vanguards professional revolutionaries or student activists.

If contemporary identity politics does, in fact, break with the class-based "identity politics" of Marxism and Marx-inspired theory, then the break is found here. Consider, for example, the relatively recent "Black Feminist Statement" of the Combahee River Collective, which Alcoff considers the "locus classicus" of contemporary identity politics, and which asserts as a matter of strategy that the best and most consistent advocate for ending the oppression of a particular identity group is that group itself.[7] This seemingly commonsense claim (and to some extent the very existence of such a statement) belies Habermas's claim that structural transformation must come from within the ranks of the privileged. Of course, the continued oppression of the very identity group represented by this black feminist Collective prevents us from deeming it a complete success, and so makes evaluating Habermas's claim about *successful* transformation more difficult. Such a definitive falsification would involve specifying "structural transformation" in a more precise way, a project that would not get one very far at any rate, since both Habermas and the members of such a Collective would probably agree that neither privileged nor underprivileged groups have as yet achieved that weighty task.

Still, there is certainly some evidence that the civil rights movement, to take one example of "underprivileged" identity-based political movements, brought about important transformations, at least in the legal structure, even if these successes are in new danger of being dismantled by neoliberal "reforms."[8] Similarly, the feminist movement brought about wide-ranging transformations in the legal system as well as in civil society, such that Habermas, in his later writings, often holds up the "feminist politics of equality" as a model for a transformational identity politics. Yet these writings show a continued hesitance to ascribe the same capacity for transformation to "cultural and ethnic minorities," perhaps for some of the same reasons elucidated in "Technology and Science as Ideology."[9] This is not to say that women are not oppressed or "underprivileged" as a group, but, as Habermas implies and recent feminism acknowledges, since women are present in every group and level of society, they may be privileged in some respects (for example, as *white* women) while nonetheless oppressed in others. However, insofar as this is also true of most (if not all) other identity groups (for example, men enjoy the privileges of sexism and male supremacy even within oppressed groups), it does not justify a conceptual distinction between women and other "minorities."

Rather, there are more compelling reasons to be hesitant about identity politics as it is straightforwardly set out by the Collective's Statement and the many other groups that followed their example, reasons that overlap with perhaps the most common objection to identity politics generally. This objection fears that linking politics to identity may undermine the potential for a shared solidarity around issues of (in)justice, reinforce illegitimate social divisions, and generally "balkanize" society in ways that at best problematize democratic decision making and at worst give rise to violent clashes between identity groups.[10] More than remnants of Leninist vanguardism, it is probably this worry that inspires the mature Habermas's hesitance about certain kinds of identity politics, mirrored in his objections to Westphalianism and the traditional conception of the absolute sovereignty of nation-states understood as "peoples." In recent work, Habermas rejects the understanding of political membership as derived from a strong collective identity, be it ethnic, national, or even mythical.[11] He sees such a view of the polity, which undergirds the traditional conception of the nation-state (at least in origin) as "inextricably bound up with the Machiavellian will to self-assertion by which the conduct of sovereign states in the arena of the "great powers" had been guided from the beginning."[12] That is, a conception of politics that makes identity a requirement for political inclusion risks substituting a reified, insular, and ultimately arbitrary homogeneity for the "higher-level intersubjectivity of a discursive agreement between citizens who recognize one another as free and equal."[13] At worst, such a conception risks relegating the political other to the status of mortal enemy à la Carl Schmitt, against whom the most extreme forms of violence can be perpetrated.[14]

These are serious concerns, as the atrocities committed by the Third Reich as well as more recent waves of genocide and ethnic violence continue to demonstrate. But do such lethal dangers really lie beneath the surface of the seemingly simple claim that the oppressed themselves are the staunchest opponents of their own oppression? The applicability of the criticism to contemporary identity politics (as opposed to allegedly sovereign nation-states or historically insular and xenophobic political movements) relies upon at least two assumptions, both of which turn out to be false: (1) Identity itself is static, and not a product of the "higher-level intersubjectivity" embodied in discursive deliberation; and (2) The elimination of their own oppression is the *sole* objective of oppressed identity groups, an objective that is not linked in any way to a larger concern for social justice and "structural transformation."

Regarding 1, few serious social theorists would still hold that identities, collective or personal, are determined by biology, anthropology, history, or other "objective" factors.[15] Rather, it has become commonly accepted that identity is "socially constructed," though there is no little confusion over the exact meaning of this fashionable phrase.[16] At minimum, social constructivism about identity asserts that collective identities such as race, gender, ethnicity, nationality, and so on are not biological or historical facts, but social categories that are more or less actively constructed and reconstructed by human beings acting in concert. The qualification "more or less," however, points to a crucial ambiguity in this general description. Namely, it does not say *how* human beings acting in concert construct their identities, nor does it specify the extent to which such a process is constrained or unconstrained, just or unjust. So, though one might see constructivism as similar to what I have called intentionalism, there is actually an important difference. Intentionalism implies that collective identities are socially constructed *by the group members themselves*, while constructivism in general allows for the possibility that collective identities are constructed in other ways, including ways that make certain groups experience their collective identity as imposed and constraining. So, a non-intentionalist approach to group membership and collective identity can still be constructivist, as I will demonstrate shortly.

Additionally, social constructivism often asserts that personal identity is not simply reducible to collective identity, such that one cannot deduce personality characteristics like timidity, intelligence, or sexual prowess from the "fact" that an individual is a member of a certain racial or gender category. Rather, individuals construct their personal identity in part by interpreting, adopting, or rejecting their group memberships. It appears initially that these two levels of construction are conceptually separable. One might think it possible to hold, for example, that "man" and "woman" are somehow natural or biological categories, but still reject the stereotypes traditionally attached to gender roles, acknowledging that these roles are based on contingent cultural values rather than biological facts. Conversely, one might hold that such social categories are thoroughly fictitious, yet maintain that they have gained such wide acceptance that they nonetheless limit the ability of individuals to accept or reject them.[17] For example, one might think that though race is socially constructed, it does not follow that individuals in racially categorized societies can simply choose not to be the race that has been ascribed to them.[18] That is, one could hold that *personal* identity is socially constructed insofar as persons construct it from available collective identities, some of which might *not* themselves be socially constructed, but natural, biological, and so on. Or, one could hold that *collective* identities are socially constructed, but that they can, in certain cases, fully determine the personal identities of those that they purport to describe.

One can see, then, that beyond the rejection of fully deterministic accounts of identity, social constructivism lends itself to a wide variety of interpretations, from postmodern accounts that see the construction of one's self as an ethical or aesthetic project undertaken by individuals, to structural accounts that find the collective identities artificially imposed by systems of power just as constraining as identities "determined" by biology, anthropology, and so forth. However, when social constructivism takes the fact of oppression seriously, it must admit that the spectrum of opportunities and constraints involved in constructing identity is not uniform across all groups. The postmodern vision of identity construction as a liberating ethical or aesthetic project may be a more apt description of how *privileged* groups willfully construct their own identities; but for oppressed groups, their socially constructed identities may nonetheless be experienced as external limitations or constraints. This is because, as noted above, social constructivism is often less than clear about *who* is doing the constructing, let alone about the political ramifications of that question. In the previous chapters, I have distinguished ascriptive from intentional (self-ascriptive) identities, and argued that oppression consists in the attempt to eliminate self-ascription leading to group harm. The point to make here is that even ascriptive identities can be understood as socially constructed; in short, that "socially constructed" does not automatically translate into "freely" or "intentionally constructed." Again, the latter must be understood as a characteristic of *privileged* groups. Indeed, part of the reason for distinguishing retributive and democratic identity politics is to emphasize this insight.

The discursive interpretation I will propose has the further advantage of specifying the relation between the construction of personal identity and the construction of collective identity. In short, *intersubjectivity* provides the link between these two interpretive poles. Insofar as the construction of personal identity takes place within a context of social relations—that is, insofar as the idea we develop of ourselves is shaped by others—it is already a collective process. Likewise, the personal identities taken on by individual group members also shape the collective identity of the group(s) to which they belong. Black presidents, female soldiers, gay athletes, and other individuals have slowly transformed the very idea of what it means to be a member of certain identity groups, and what such groups are capable of. Under normal (that is, ideal) circumstances, this reciprocal process of collective and personal identity formation is not necessarily political. This is why Habermas characterizes private autonomy, including, for example, individual choices about what type of life to pursue, as entitlements to "suspend" or "drop out" of communicative action contexts.[19] However, under oppressive conditions, the strategic political program of oppressed groups may include intentionally guiding members to pursue certain private goals, as exemplified by certain kinds of minority scholarships aimed at placing group members in occupations where they are traditionally underrepresented. This is a further example of how collective and personal identity mutually shape one another.

I will describe this discursive conception of identity formation in greater detail in the following section. For now, I mean primarily to point out that the construction of identity *is* (or at least can be) a result of a "higher level intersubjectivity," a fact that Habermas recognizes by describing identity in terms of "ethical-cultural discourses" (see chapter 2). So, the rejection of identity politics for fear of balkanization and lack of democratic solidarity turns out to be unwarranted. In the end, group differences pose no greater threat to democratic practice then individual differences, since both ideally arise from the same intersubjective processes. This does not mean that all identity groups are open and inclusive, any more than all individuals are tolerant and law abiding. Both claims are easily disproved on empirical grounds alone. However, from the fact that some identities may be problematic for democratic societies, it does not follow that identity itself is a problematic concept. On the contrary, the need to distinguish between "good" and "bad" identity politics calls for a more nuanced theory of identity that recognizes the complexity of identity and the multiplicity of its ways of relating—healthy and unhealthy—to the general polity.

The second assumption underlying worries about balkanization and separatism mirrors certain standard criticisms of social contract theory and its basis in individual "rational" egoism. Such criticisms point out that the overlapping self-interest in security of person and property that alleges to be the rational foundation for political authority is, in fact, a mere modus vivendi, too weak and strategic to provide lasting political stability.[20] Such a minimal agreement would risk collapsing as soon as one or some of the parties to it found sufficient strength and resources to bend it to their own advantage. Similarly, opponents of identity politics fear that the picture of identity groups concerned solely or even primarily with their own oppression marks a return to a "state of nature" type politics of warring factions, only now with groups rather than individuals as its fundamental actors. Such critics may nonetheless sympathize with the project of eliminating oppression. Yet they see a wider coalition around injustice generally as the necessary democratic foundation for such a project, a foundation they think is undermined by those who would limit solidarity to members of one's identity group.

Such a criticism raises important concerns, but it caricatures serious conceptions of identity politics. For one, few if any proponents of identity politics oppose developing wider political coalitions, nor do they reject support and solidarity from outsiders. The Combahee River Collective, for example, espoused a commitment to a fairly orthodox Marxist revolutionary agenda in addition to their particular "self-interested" concern for ending their own oppression. Their commitment to fighting for their own liberation was in the first place a simple recognition of the fact that outside support and solidarity for their cause was sorely lacking, rather than unwelcome. Secondly, their Statement must be understood in opposition to an orthodoxy that held that racism, sexism, and other identity-based injustices must be subjugated to class-based injustice, and were therefore best addressed "after the revolution." To the contrary, they believed that a successful revolutionary movement must first overcome false, ideological divisions within the ranks of the proletariat, divisions based upon race, gender, sexuality, and so on, effectively reversing the priority of identity and class-based struggles.

However, even this simplification is misleading, since the relationship between "self-interested" identity politics and a more general politics of liberation is not a question of temporal or even conceptual priority. Rather, if one understands oppression in the way that I have described it, collective struggles for self-ascription are both self-interested and socially progressive. That is, the analogy between the self-interest of classical liberalism's prepolitical individuals and the "self-interest" of oppressed groups in oppressive societies breaks down once the democratic character of struggles for self-ascription is made clear. Insofar as self-ascription is a general requirement for a flourishing democracy, particular struggles to that end already coincide with a more general interest in social justice in a way that the private pursuit of individual self-interest (which in any case, in the classical liberal tradition, usually amounts to the quest for private property) does not.

Lani Guinier and Gerald Torres demonstrate this point nicely in their book *The Miner's Canary*, in which they argue that racial identity represents a barometer of sorts for the health of American democracy generally. Their apt metaphor is worth quoting at length:

> Miners often carried a canary into the mine alongside them. The canary's more fragile respiratory system would cause it to collapse from noxious gases long before humans were affected, thus alerting the miners to danger. The canary's distress signaled that it was time to get out of the mine because the air was becoming too poisonous to breathe. Those who are racially marginalized are like the miner's canary: their distress is the first sign of a danger that threatens us all. It is easy enough to think that when we sacrifice this canary, the only harm is to communities of color. Yet others ignore this problem at their own peril, for these problems are symptoms warning us that we are all at risk.[21]

Part of the risk that Guinier and Torres point to is the risk of oppression: the risk that ascriptive identification will come to plague all identity groups, and not just racial minorities; a risk that is demonstrated, for example, in the difficulties and identity crises often experienced by progressive white youths who wish to affirm a positive, yet antiracist white identity.[22] Racial identity thus has a "diagnostic function" as a locus for gauging the health of democracy generally. But their conception of racial identity is also "activist" insofar as it uses "collective identity as a site for democratic participation," a political strategy that they find worthy of generalization.[23] Thus political activism coalesces around "race" (understood as a set of political concerns typically associated with people deemed "racial minorities," rather than biologically or otherwise deterministically) but comes to include other groups as well, insofar as its goals are vital to the practice of democracy generally. In short, Guinier and Torres demonstrate that struggles against racial oppression are always already struggles for social justice generally, insofar as the goals they pursue "self-interestedly" are, in reality, in the interest of everyone (or at least, the vast majority of us).

What we have, then, is a precise inversion of Habermas's claim that structural transformation must come from the ranks of the privileged (a claim that he no longer defends at any rate, as demonstrated by his admission that feminism and other kinds of identity politics play a crucial role in transforming public debate and expanding exclusionary public spheres), and a defense of a certain kind of inclusive identity politics (though Guinier and Torres do not use that term) that is not just a politics of competing, collective self-interests. I will discuss race and racial identity explicitly in the following chapter. For now I only mean to point out that conceptions of identity politics worth taking seriously need not lead to balkanization and separatism, nor need they be elitist or vanguard. The point is simple enough: Underprivileged identity groups can and do represent a "conflict zone" capable of structural transformation, as they are well (and perhaps even best) suited to fight oppression in the interest of democracy, in part since the force of this kind of injustice is felt by them most directly, and by no means in an abstract way. It remains to be seen whether identity would continue to be the locus of political action under ideal democratic conditions.

DISCURSIVE-DEMOCRATIC IDENTITY POLITICS

The previous section analyzed identity politics as a strategy for fighting oppression. As such, it falls under the rubric of nonideal theory, an enterprise that has been sorely neglected at least since the dominance of the Rawlsian paradigm in Anglo-American political philosophy. One may grant everything that was said there, and nonetheless maintain that in an ideal, nonoppressive democracy, identity would be irrelevant to the practice of democracy. In fact, such a claim often motivates the negligence of issues of oppression and other injustices in mainstream political theory. Moreover, even those who do address certain kinds of identity (namely cultural identity) in political terms, such as Kymlicka and other multicultural liberals, rely on a distinction between ideal and nonideal theory in order to justify excluding other kinds of identity (namely racial, gender, and other "disadvantaged" identities) that they think would no longer be relevant in ideal democracies. I have previously argued that such exclusions are unjustified.[24] Yet, such theorists are right at least that, in a more just world, identity would relate to politics in a different, less agonistic way. In what follows, I will outline how that relation might be understood.

In the first place, it is necessary to understand that the scope of ideal theory is contestable. In order to be useful, ideal theories must paint a picture of society that is actually achievable, or at least closely imitable. They must be, to use Rawls's term, "realistically utopian."[25] Accordingly, even an ideal society will be confronted with problems related to immigration, disability, individual prejudice, crime, and so on.[26] Some individuals will be better off and others worse. And collective identity will presumably still play a key role in how individuals understand themselves and their political interests. The crucial difference is that, in an ideal democracy, these problems and social facts would be dealt with in a fairer, more democratic way, such that the "least well off," again to use a Rawlsian phrase, would not include a disproportionate number of any one identity group, nor would it involve the kind of debilitating and systematic poverty one sees today. Nor would immigration favor some identities over others, criminal law treat members of one group differently from others, and so on. In other words, one's life chances would not be significantly determined by one's group memberships and collective identities. It does not follow, however, that identity would cease to be politically salient.

So how would identity function under ideal democratic conditions? That is, what kinds of collective identities would such conditions produce and/or accommodate? One way to begin such an analysis is negatively, by ruling out certain kinds of identities. Most theorists of democracy agree that not all collective identities will be acceptable. Rawls admits, for example, that though an overlapping consensus on basic principles of political organization, he thinks, would be acceptable to the vast majority of "comprehensive doctrines," it can (or must) nonetheless legitimately exclude certain extreme views that are incompatible with the idea of society as system of social cooperation.[27] Similarly, Habermas acknowledges that even an appropriately democratic constitutional state, one that assured equal rights and participation as well as provided due recognition to "minority cultures" and other historically underrepresented (or, as I prefer, oppressed) groups, can (or must) nonetheless legitimately exclude "fundamentalist" groups that refuse to acknowledge basic principles of freedom and equality.[28] And in a different, but related, vein, David Ingram argues that the affirmation of white identity is an illegitimate form of identity politics, since it is bound up with unjust privileges and a history of domination in ways that "subaltern" identities are not.[29] At some level, these claims mean to circumscribe the limits of liberal toleration. Yet, just as much, they assert that certain collective identities are unacceptable in democratic societies; that they have no legitimate claim to recognition. Such a claim cannot be arbitrary. It must be guided by some principle or set of principles that explains why some collective identities are worthy of recognition while others are not.

Further, in light of the assertion by defenders of identity politics that, though some identity politics are inimical to democracy, not *all* are, such a set of principles will be the same that allow one to distinguish "good" identity politics from "bad." I submit that, just as the discourse principle can be "operationalized" in the spheres of morality and law, it can also be applied to the "ethical-cultural" sphere, providing a speculative picture of what identity politics might look like under ideal conditions. Here one must proceed cautiously. I do not mean to suggest that government, or for that matter philosophy, has any legitimate role in collective identity formation. It is not the job of the state or the philosopher to police identities. However, even an ideal democracy must have some nonarbitrary means of determining its legitimate constituency. As Schmittean political theorists have aptly pointed out, a completely inclusive democracy would not only be empirically implausible but is actually a self-contradictory idea.[30] Democracy, by definition, involves the constitution of a people, or demos, that understands itself in part by distinguishing itself from outsiders. Yet one need not take this to mean that the process by which such a body is constituted is somehow beyond morality, legality, or reason. The essence of Habermas's alternative to such a radical decisionism lies in the claim that the constitution of the demos can itself be legitimated democratically, if only in a retroactive way.

As chapter 2 demonstrated, this process of legitimation is embodied, on the one hand, in formal democratic institutions that transform public opinion into the rule of law; and on the other hand, in an informal public sphere fueled, in part, by identity politics. Under nonideal conditions, where oppression still structures social and political life (what I have called "retributive"), identity politics has the dual function of reinterpreting collective identity internally, combating negative stereotypes and replacing them with a positive group image, and expanding the scope of equality externally, through political action oriented toward a wider public sphere. The former function is what Habermas calls "self-clarification," while the latter represents the potential for "structural transformation" inherent in this kind of discourse. To note this "dual function," however, is not to suggest that the two activities are distinct or separate in practice (such that first a group clarifies its identity, *then* it engages in action oriented toward wider publics; or that it could have a subgroup or committee dedicated to self-clarification and a subgroup or committee dedicated to external political action). Rather, the activity of self-clarification itself effects changes in society at large, just as it depends in certain ways upon the recognition of those outside the group. Still, the conceptual distinction is coherent and useful, and further, it seems plausible to think that under non-oppressive conditions the self-clarification function might be "uncoupled" to some extent from the structural transformation function. This does not mean that collective identities would become completely independent and self-sufficient, but only that the construction and exploration of identity would not have to simultaneously fight for its very preconditions. Thus all group identities would be constructed under the conditions of a "communicative freedom" that is already enjoyed by privileged groups. I have conceived such a freedom, as it applies to *groups*, as a *right to self-ascription*, and argued that such a right is foundational, in a certain sense, for individual rights. For oppressed groups, the denial of this basic right is in large part what gives moral weight to their struggles for recognition. Indeed, though the mantra "by any means necessary" may be a slight rhetorical exaggeration, the severely disabling character of oppression may in fact justify political tactics that would, under normal conditions, be unjustifiable.[31]

Yet what justificatory force remains for identity politics once oppression is eliminated and the right to self-ascription is universally actualized? The answer is that identity politics is inevitable, even under ideal conditions. Group membership is the medium through which one first sees oneself as a political being, one whose associations with others can be collectively organized and regulated. And so it is not surprising that it is as members of groups that individuals develop their particular political consciousness, and that it is groups rather than individuals that are most influential in political processes. Such a statement is fairly uncontroversial if one thinks first of *interest* groups: political parties, lobbyists, voluntary associations, and so on. Yet, as Amy Gutmann suggests, "people's interests and understanding of their interests are just as identity-driven as their identities are interest driven."[32] As described in the previous chapter, it is only within the context of collective identity that individuation (and so also the construction of an individual "interest" or political orientation) can develop. Identity, then, is an irreducible feature of democratic political practice. Yet, it does not follow that any and all identities must be equally recognized and respected.

In terms of a legitimate coercive mechanism, all that can be *required* of collective identities is that they assent to basic constitutional principles. Thus all identities would be bound together by this "weak constitutional patriotism." Yet beyond this basic condition (and beyond the cautious proceduralism that Habermas's mature thought expresses), the seeds of a radical, emancipatory social ideal still link Habermas's discourse theory with his earliest attempts to theorize genuinely human interests. Thus, even though Habermas repeatedly emphasizes that questions of ethics (and thus ethical-cultural identities) are *not* subject to the same process of universal justification as questions of morality, justice, and law, when an interviewer asked him if he thought that, in an ideal society, ethical questions of the good and moral questions of the right would overlap, he answered in the affirmative, if somewhat tentatively.[33] This suggests that the discourse ethic may indeed provide a picture of how groups would construct their identity under ideal conditions, even if such a picture is largely speculative. One might even continue to call such a picture "normative," if one could imagine a noncoercive normativity, the sense of which would be more akin to the psychoanalytic sense of "normal" or "typical" rather than the objectively moral sense of "binding" or "enforceable." Such an extension of discourse theory in a (realistically) utopian direction seems to me consistent with what Habermas himself has characterized as a continuous research program uniting all of his work, a program that aims to locate in human reason a radical, universal potential for liberating us from domination in general and organizing *all* aspects of our lives in a (communicatively) rational way. To use Habermas's own words, "discourse ethics, though organized around a concept of procedure, can be expected to say something relevant about substance as well and, more important perhaps, about the hidden link between justice and the common good."[34] What follows is an attempt to illuminate this link without collapsing its poles and without denying the plurality of collective identities (and so, conceptions of the good) even under ideal conditions.

The discourse ethic finds a norm valid insofar as it "could meet with the agreement of all those concerned in their capacity as participants in a practical discourse."[35] Habermas specifies such an agreement by way of four pragmatic rules of discourse:

1. Nobody who could make a relevant contribution may be excluded (the inclusiveness condition).
2. All participants are granted an equal opportunity to make contributions (the equality condition).
3. The participants must mean what they say (the sincerity condition).
4. Communication must be freed from external and internal coercion so that the . . . stances that participants take on criticizable validity claims are motivated solely by the rational force of the better reasons (the freedom condition).[36]

In applying these principles to the process of (ethical) identity formation, the first principle goes to the heart of the matter, though it certainly does not settle it, since the determination of whose contributions are relevant circumscribes group membership. That is, the relevant contributions to a conception of collective identity are those that come from the "inside," from members themselves.[37] This is the very meaning of self-ascription. However, this does not mean the principle is unproblematic, as internal conflicts over who counts as a full-fledged member of a group (and so whose contributions are relevant) are common and provide no shortage of difficult examples for theorists of group rights and sovereignty. Consider, for example, the case of *Santa Clara Pueblo v. Martinez*, in which a Pueblo woman brought suit against her tribe for its practice of denying tribal membership and its benefits to the children of women who marry outside of the tribe, while extending membership and its benefits to the children of men who marry outside of the tribe. The final Supreme Court decision on the matter, which upheld the sovereignty of the tribe in determining its membership even to the point of discriminating against its female members, may seem to be in line with what I have called the right to self-ascription. Yet in actuality the self-ascription of one group—the Pueblo tribe—is bought at the price of the self-ascription of another—women—whose ability to construct their collective identity in positive terms is undermined by practices such as these.[38] So the right to self-ascription cannot provide a definitive answer to conflicts like these. Rather, as I have previously suggested, such conflicts must be adjudicated on a case by case basis. However, when "insiders" petition the government to intervene on behalf of an *internally* oppressed group, the extent to which the groups in question approximate the discursive ideal of identity construction (for example, the extent to which they take seriously the "equality" and "freedom" conditions of discourse) can be taken into account when choosing which identity group to favor. This way of balancing the interests of different groups in cases where some decision *must* be made, and where even inaction amounts to favoring one conception over another, differs from externally coercing groups to be or be seen a certain way.

Multicultural liberals focus especially on cases like this because they think that, unlike problems of affirmative action, reparations, and other temporary group concerns, conflicts between the values of sovereign "national minorities" and "our own" liberal values of freedom and equality are inevitable, even in ideal multicultural states.[39] They take such conflicts, then, to be something like pure problems of ideal political theory, as ineluctable in the realm of politics as Kant's antinomies in the realm of metaphysics. Yet often this is far from the truth. In fact, as I argued in the first chapter, the cultural conflicts that multicultural liberalism takes as paradigmatic are often just as subject to historical contingency as those it dismisses as problems of nonideal theory. In the *Martinez* case, for example, it has been argued that the subjugation of women was in part codified by earlier federal laws which modeled certain misogynist structures present in the *majority* culture and its legal system.[40] Far from being an authentic expression of tribal sovereignty, then, the exclusion of women may be seen in part as an adoption of external attitudes and practices leading to oppression (in Habermasian terms, a colonization of the lifeworld). Thus taking sides in such "internal" conflicts no longer appears as cultural imperialism, but as a way of rectifying our own past injustices.

My point here is that difficult cases like these may not be as enduring as some theorists imagine them to be, and that, under more ideal circumstances, when groups are truly left to construct their own identity without coercion, the results would normally meet the criteria listed above. To be clear, this is a descriptive claim but one with normative significance. If groups do have a right to self-ascription as I have argued, and if we have a picture of what it would look like to exercise that right, then that picture becomes "regulative" in the sense that it can show us whether current identity constructions are nearer or further from the ideal.[41] This claim is also difficult to confirm, given its speculative nature and the lack of empirical evidence available. However, I believe its validity can be determined by the following premises:

   1. Persons, as language users, strive to reach understanding with one another.
   2. Intersubjectivity provides the context within which such understanding can be reached.
   3. Coercion and "colonization" inhibit the capacity to reach understanding. And therefore:
   4. Groups that coerce their members will be rejected by them, provided other intersubjective contexts are available.

The first two premises are central to Habermas's theory of communicative action, which demonstrates that linguistic understanding is possible only against the background of certain normative assumptions, understood as "validity claims" to truth, sincerity, and rightness.[42] This means that communication itself presupposes the possibility of normative agreement—that linguistic meaning is inseparable from the intersubjective context in which it is produced through communication. From this foundational linguistic competency, Habermas deduces the potential for rationally guiding our collective lives and the social, political, and economic systems that (ideally) facilitate such a task, through collective, communicative action. However, as I illustrated in chapter 2, when unregulated by communicative "steering mechanisms," these systems "colonize the lifeworld" and impede its ability to create meaning and reach understanding, thus becoming coercive rather than (communicatively) rational. This is the meaning of the third premise, which sees successful communication and coercion as mutually exclusive. One can conclude from these premises that groups that do not provide the communicative resources for creating meaning (for the present purpose, the meaning of being an "X," that is, collective identity) will tend to be abandoned by their members, provided that other intersubjective contexts for identity formation are available.

This last proviso is important, as it explains why, in reality, group members often *do not* abandon their groups, even when they fail to meet the discursive criteria listed above. In many cases, no alternative contexts exist for internally oppressed groups to construct positive alternative identities, so they remain within collectivities that may be debilitating. That individuals may refuse to exit groups that constrain them even to the point of violating their rights further demonstrates the importance and even unavoidability of group membership. Yet group members may choose not to leave oppressive groups for other reasons as well. Herr highlights these reasons in her account of the "insider's perspective" on minority cultures.[43] She argues that the views of "cultural insiders" must be taken seriously, even when they defend cultures that internally oppress them. Instead of seeing such a defense as false-consciousness, internalized oppression, and so on, we should recognize, she thinks, that even oppressed members often find (at least potential) value in their groups, and so are more interested in reforming it internally than outright rejecting it or opening it up to transformation from outsiders who fail to grasp the internal complexity of the culture.

Thus Herr notes the "democratic potential" of even oppressive groups, and argues that the morally justified response toward minority cultures is not to liberalize them, but "to open up and protect the channels of internal democracy so that cultural insiders are empowered to voice their differing views free from intimidation and coercion."[44] Again, the principles of discourse capture this potential nicely. That is, even if groups lack the characteristics of inclusiveness, equality, sincerity, and freedom, one might still see them as evolving toward such an ideal through internal reforms. Still, this does not contradict the conclusion that members will *eventually* abandon their groups if these reforms do not come about, or if at least some progress is not made such that one could still believe in their "democratic potential." Both possibilities, however, abandonment and reform, equally support the thesis that under ideal conditions, groups would tend to display the characteristics made explicit in the discourse ethic, since, together, they demonstrate a kind of social selection, in which groups either evolve toward an internally democratic structure or are abandoned or replaced by more democratic alternatives. One might call this the *democratic selection thesis*.

Such a thesis does, however, contradict the claim that groups or "cultures" have a general right to survival, regardless of how they are viewed by others, or even by their own members. Against Taylor, who defends this claim most eloquently, Habermas argues that governments should not and even *cannot* guarantee the survival of any particular group.[45] This is, first of all, because successful collective identities are inevitably confronted by changing circumstances—modernization, immigration, environmental crises, and so forth—to which they must adapt. Healthy collective identities are thus constantly being reinterpreted and transformed by their members such that they remain relevant and useful as contexts for individuation. Collectivities that fail to adapt in this way pay the price of irrelevance and eventual extinction. Yet "to guarantee survival would necessarily rob the members of the very freedom to say yes or no that is necessary if they are to appropriate and preserve their cultural heritage."[46] It would, in other words, fail to satisfy the fourth rule of discourse, the freedom condition. That is, governments can protect collective identities that are valued by their members, but they cannot force members to value particular collective identities. Doing so would involve the same kind of coercion that makes forced assimilation, official disrespect, discrimination, and other state interventions in collective identity normatively reprehensible.

In addition to a lack of alternative intersubjective contexts and the desire for internal reform, there is at least one more important factor for understanding why groups fail to embody the discursive principles listed above, namely, the lack of *material* resources: poverty, unemployment, economic crisis, and other "traditional" concerns of leftist, labor-oriented politics. This concern for the material bases of abstract rights has sometimes been presented in opposition to "recognition" based theories like Honneth's and (perhaps) Habermas's, and also to identity politics in general. In the following section, then, I will address this concern and argue that identity politics can and does encapsulate concerns of distributive justice as well as recognition of collective identity. Before beginning this analysis, however, it is necessary to address what I have called the sincerity condition of discourse and its relation to collective identity formation.

The requirement that discursive participants must mean what they say may seem strange, not least because insincerity seems much more difficult to identify, let alone prohibit, than inequality, exclusion, or coercion. Yet it makes more sense, again, if one views it as a description of uninhibited identity construction rather than a prohibition. That is, under circumstances of oppression, there are many reasons why groups might take a strategic, rather than sincere (or, to use a dangerous term, authentic) stance toward their collective identity. In the first place, they might outright refuse to elaborate their collective identity in the terms available in public discourse. Ingram's point that such a "refusal to enter into the established discourse may well represent a principled moral stance against oppression and injustice" applies just as well to ethical-cultural discourses as moral ones, especially when the "established discourses" caricature a group's identity in harmful ways.[47] Secondly, oppressed groups are sometimes forced to construct their identities reactively, in ways that combat harmful stereotypes, but these (re)constructions may well be strategic, and just as "essentializing" as those they mean to combat. For example, even Kwame Anthony Appiah, who vehemently rejects "race" as a false and useless concept, nonetheless recognizes that "racial identity" cannot simply be done away with for the purposes of political action.[48] Rather, it is something that must be used strategically and even "ironically" until it is no longer necessary: that is, until oppression is eliminated and collective identity can be constructed *sincerely*, without concern for how it may function strategically.

Finally, the phenomenon of "passing" also provides a good example of how oppressive conditions may sometimes require insincerity. While the individual motivations for passing surely vary, some oppressed individuals who "pass" as white, straight, Christian, and so on presumably do so to avoid some of the hardships associated with being or being seen as who they "really" are.[49] Without delving too deeply into this complex issue, it is clear at least that, where the negative consequences of being a member of a certain group are eliminated, the strategic motivation to conceal one's membership in that group is also. This is why the sincerity condition is included in the features of identity construction under ideal circumstances. By no means, however, does this condition require constructing an ideal of authenticity to which groups or their members can be held accountable, an undertaking which is problematic at best. Having described this and the other conditions in some detail, then, let me now move on to the analysis of the *material* conditions for self-ascription, and the objections raised by those who see identity politics as insufficiently attentive to those conditions.

MISRECOGNITION AND MATERIAL DEPRIVATION

By understanding oppression in terms of the denial of the right to self-ascription, and (retributive) identity politics as the struggle to actualize this right, one might think that I have missed something crucial about oppression. Namely, one might object that oppression often if not always involves material deprivation: inequalities in income, wealth, and in accessing vital resources like education, health care, adequate housing, and so on. One might object, in other words, that I have not accounted for distributive injustice as a feature of oppression. Admittedly, I have not discussed the distribution of resources in great detail. However, this is because I believe that the distributive inequalities experienced by oppressed groups are conceptually separate from oppression itself. In other words, it is not because they experience distributive inequality that oppressed groups are oppressed. Rather, oppression makes groups vulnerable to economic exploitation and distributive injustice. Certainly the converse is true as well: economic exploitation and distributive injustice make groups (and individuals, since groups are no longer necessarily fundamental for understanding issues of distribution, or at least, my arguments up to now do not entail this claim) vulnerable to oppression. Yet this is no reason to conflate the two phenomena. Somewhat similarly, Nancy Fraser argues that distributive injustice and "misrecognition" are conceptually distinct, even if they are often empirically linked.[50] I disagree with her claim, however, that identity politics, as I understand it, is insufficient for addressing the distributive injustices associated with oppression.

In her exchange with Honneth, Fraser argues that a suitable approach to issues of social justice must employ a "perspectival dualism."[51] It must, as I have done above, attempt to identify the "intersubjective" conditions of just social organization: the conditions of reciprocity and mutual respect that make possible substantive equality. On the other hand, it must also identify the "objective" conditions of just social organization, including, most importantly, just distribution of the material resources necessary to make formal political rights effective and actionable. While these two perspectives tend toward different "folk paradigms" of justice—the recognition-based identity politics of the "new social movements" on the one hand, and the traditional distribution-based politics of labor on the other—Fraser recognizes that in reality, most if not all social justice movements can and should be understood as making both distributive and recognition-based demands. Thus, her perspectival dualism suggests that *all* social injustices should be analyzed from *both* perspectives simultaneously, rather than using the language of recognition for some and the language of redistribution for others, and without subsuming one perspective under another in a reductive fashion.

I fully agree, and this is why, though oppression may often entail distributive injustice (in some cases fulfilling the definitional requirement "leading to group harm") and vice versa, I have taken care to keep the two conceptually distinct. I disagree, however, with Fraser's estimation of identity politics as necessarily reducing issues of justice to issues of recognition, and thereby neglecting distributive injustice or, as she puts it "conspir[ing] to decenter, if not extinguish, claims for egalitarian redistribution."[52] This claim is mistaken both empirically and conceptually. In the first place, the empirical claim that identity politics has somehow eclipsed redistributive politics is misleading, since most identity-based movements, from Black Nationalism, to feminism, to the struggles of indigenous "national minorities" have given a central place to concerns over distribution. Alcoff provides an extensive list of such identity-based political movements and their demands for redistribution:

> African American political organizations like the NAACP and the Black Radical Congress have called for reparations for slavery; women's organizations like NOW have demanded an end to gender-based pay inequities; and NARAL (the National Abortion Rights Action League) has demanded access to abortion for poor women. The National Council of La Raza has organized for welfare rights, home loans for Latinos, and improvement of public schools, and the National Gay and Lesbian Task Force has fought for an end to job and housing discrimination and universal access to AIDS medication as well as health insurance for domestic partners.[53]

Even the civil rights movement, with its assimilationist aims and its focus on equal *recognition* under the law, nonetheless gave central place to distributive claims.[54] Far from "decentering" claims for redistribution then, identity-based political groups like those above would seem to bring them into sharper relief, if only because they see themselves, as the Black Feminist Collective did, as the most dedicated advocates for such claims.

Further, even though I have focused on ascriptive identification (what Fraser and Honneth would call "misrecognition") as the antithesis of the right to self-ascription, it does not follow that such an approach cannot also identify distributive and/or material impediments to self-ascription. For one, the group harm characteristic of oppression derives as much from material deprivation as from stereotypes, insults, and other less tangible harms. Indeed, part of what makes undeserved material inequalities morally egregious is that they devalue one's sense of worth. When considering inequalities between groups, then—say, wage disparities between men and women, or whites and blacks—part of what makes these inequalities unjust is that they unjustly devalue group identities. One of Honneth's central theses is that, as a matter of empirical fact, most often it is this experience of disrespect that fuels social struggles, rather than material necessity. I think Honneth's empirical/phenomenological claim here is correct. Still, it is not necessary to reduce distributive injustices to their phenomenological basis in misrecognition, as he does, in order to defend identity politics in my sense. That is, identity politics may be important and defensible even if the development of an intact identity is not the *fundamental* goal of normative politics, as Honneth asserts. There is nothing contradictory about defending a conception of identity politics and simultaneously recognizing that some injustices may have nothing to do with misrecognition, or that the ability to develop an intact identity may have *material* as well as social and psychological prerequisites.[55] In fact, insofar as certain identity groups may have disproportionate experiences of distributive injustice, it is not surprising that concerns for redistribution are often brought into the public eye through the lens of identity.

The perspective of distribution also helps to identify deviations from discursive-democratic identity formation other than those discussed above. That is, unjust patterns of distribution may explain why groups fail to embody the principles of discourse even if other intersubjective contexts are available to their members, and even if the groups and their members have little interest in internal reforms in the interest of greater inclusiveness, equality, and so on. Consider, for example, neo-Nazi skinheads. Given that such groups have arisen mostly in diverse urban settings in England and the United States, it would be implausible to suggest that no alternative contexts for collective identity formation were available to their members. It is equally implausible, in my opinion, that such groups hold any promise for becoming more inclusive and democratic, since their beliefs are fundamentally inimical to democratic principles of freedom and equality.[56] One might think, then, that the existence of such groups provides a counterexample to what I have called democratic selection. However, if one looks at that group from the perspective of material distribution, the reasons for the deviation become clearer. Rather than any preexisting racial animosity, sociologists have found that the reasons young whites join racist skinhead groups are largely the same as the reasons why urban youths join gangs in general: unemployment or lack of meaningful work, lack of quality education, abusive or neglectful upbringing, and so on.[57] In fact, the first "skins" expressed no racial ideology at all, being primarily a movement in fashion and music.[58] It was only against the background of increasing unemployment, combined with new waves of immigrants willing to work for lower wages, that the skinhead movement became aligned with the racist, nationalist ideology of the National Front, among other ideologues, through the familiar scapegoating that misplaces blame for structural deficiencies on vulnerable identity groups.

I presume, then, that distributive justice would go a long way toward making hate groups like neo-Nazis irrelevant, at least insofar as it would eliminate the kinds of economic vulnerability that such groups exploit. Similarly, conflicts over scarce resources may often be prevented by eliminating the relevant material scarcity, and thus conflicts at the level of "recognition" may never arise. Concerning skinhead culture again, it is far from clear that the original movement would have developed an affinity with white supremacist ideologies against the background of full employment. At any rate, examples such as these further demonstrate the necessity of retaining an "objective" material orientation alongside intersubjective concerns for recognition. Otherwise, if one begins phenomenologically, as Honneth does, from the *experience* of misrecognition, one cannot distinguish between legitimate cases of oppression and illegitimate oppression claims (like the claim sometimes made that white men are now oppressed by minority groups) that may nonetheless be sincerely felt. I cannot address the question of what distributive arrangements would be most conducive to the right to self-ascription here, nor the larger question of what pattern or patterns of distribution are required by justice in a more general sense. I only mean to point out that the analysis I have undertaken here is not incompatible with such lines of inquiry, as Fraser and others seem to worry.

Finally, in light of my extended consideration of groups, group harm, and collective identities, one might wonder whether or how *class* membership fits within the picture of oppression that I have sketched herein. Admittedly, I have intentionally avoided this issue, in the first place because I am wary, as noted in the first chapter, of conflating significantly different kinds of harm under the umbrella term "oppression," as is often done when the term is used imprecisely. That is, insofar as the concept of class denotes some relation to economic exploitation, my intuition is that it is significantly different enough from the processes of oppression that I have described to merit separate analysis. It is not my intention to provide such an analysis here. However, I do think a few tentative points can be made, which suggest that it would not be entirely impossible to speak of something like "class oppression."

Complicating the matter somewhat is the fact that the meaning and referent of the very term "class" has come to be the subject of significant disagreement. The traditional notion of class as used by Marx, wherein one's class is determined by one's relation to the means of production, has been rendered problematic by developments in postindustrial capitalism that have created new sectors of the workforce that do not seem to fit neatly into the distinction between bourgeoisie and proletariat. Further, the rise of purely distributive, income-based understandings of class (lower class, middle class, etc.) are problematic as well, not least because they miss the fundamental conflict between classes and the exploitation of the "lower" classes by the "upper." A useful reconstruction of the concept of class must invoke qualitative as well as quantitative criteria. Fear and uncertainty about job prospects and job security, extreme dissatisfaction and despair in the face of lifelong menial labor, as well as falling wages, loss of benefits, and the increasing gap between rich and poor bind the vast majority of workers together regardless of their various relations to the means of production. Marx understood this well enough, which is why he linked the experience of (what he called) alienation to the purely material logic of capitalist exploitation. That is, the fundamental injustice of capitalism is not quantitative (that wealth is "redistributed" from the worker to the capitalist in the form of surplus value claimed as profit), but qualitative (that this distribution causes the misery of the worker, upon which the capitalist's affluence depends).[59] If such a claim is to be defended today, it seems to me that one must not lose sight of these qualitative features. And oppression, as I have defined it, may be among them. That is, the qualitative harms arising from a certain (capitalist) form of social organization might be thought to include a distinctly collective harm to a particular class (say, workers): the inability to collectively define themselves, which would entail, somewhat obviously, the right to organize trade unions and the like, but also the ability to *disband* or *reject* their group identity entirely. That is, the necessity of entering the workforce in a certain capacity, for example, as a laborer, and the harmful effects resulting from that arrangement, might be understood as a violation of the right to self-ascription, and so an instance of oppression. Again, this tentative thesis would need to be worked out in much greater detail, taking special care not to conflate oppression, exploitation, alienation and other conceptions of harm, as I have consistently warned against in the present work, and avoiding the kind of reductionism that sees class as prior to other kinds of collective identity.[60]

I take it, then, that identity politics as I have described it does not suffer from blindness to distributive injustice and material deprivation, nor from a myopic focus on issues of recognition. My claim is that identity politics plays a crucial part both in resisting oppression (retributive identity politics) and in a functioning democracy (discursive-democratic identity politics). I do not claim that it is the *only* part of those enterprises. There is room as well for theories of distributive justice, though it is not my intention to offer one. I have only aimed to show that identity politics and concerns for distribution are not incommensurable and that, in reality, they often manifest in the same social phenomena.

CONCLUSIONS AND SYNOPSIS

This and the previous two chapters represent the heart of my thesis on oppression and its remediation through identity politics justified in reference to a fundamental group right to self-ascription. I consider this approach a superior alternative to the dominant approach to collective identity and group rights, an approach I have called multicultural liberalism. The first chapter presented the critique of that approach and set out the outlines of an alternative by offering a definition of oppression and a preliminary account of the type of group right that such a definition entails. The second chapter further specified this right and argued that it must be considered foundational in a certain sense for traditional individual rights, at least insofar as such rights are interpreted discursively. This argument also coincides with and builds upon the critique of multicultural liberalism insofar as the latter employs a purely individualist approach to rights and insofar as this approach is in part what leads to an intentionalist view of group membership, with all the problems that that entails. I draw upon Habermas's discursive-democratic theory of rights because I believe that his is the best and most plausible theory available, since it preserves the best features of liberalism and communitarianism while avoiding the most serious pitfalls of either, and since, unlike many other contemporary theories of rights and democracy, it retains the potential for radical, structural transformation. I have tried to avoid a *dogmatic* Habermasianism, however, in acknowledging important criticisms of Habermas's rigorous proceduralism, especially those that point out the necessity of a *substantive* orientation toward issues of justice and morality, an orientation that Habermas frequently takes for granted. Still, I do not think such criticisms are fatal to Habermas's general project. That is, there is no contradiction involved in providing *both* procedural and substantive arguments for a right to self-ascription actualized through a certain kind of identity politics. Indeed, I take it that both perspectives are necessary since oppression undermines real-world justification procedures on the one hand, and since, on the other hand, substantive commitments are themselves constructed in a discursive fashion.

One of the chief advantages of this approach is its ability to distinguish between those groups that are worthy of respect and recognition and those that are not, based upon criteria that are, if not neutral, at least widely acceptable to the citizens and collectives that populate multicultural liberal-democracies today. These criteria too are both procedural and substantive. They are procedural insofar as they are derived and adapted from a discourse-ethical approach to *moral* justification; and they are substantive insofar as, when applied to *ethical-cultural* discourses on identity, they represent something like an intersubjective model of human flourishing, or so I have argued.

These criteria (that is, the "rules" or "principles" of discourse) may be helpful when collective identities conflict in such a way that resolution defaults to the State, but they are not best understood as coercive regulations. Rather, they provide a speculative ideal of how collective identity could be constructed under noncoercive conditions. That is, if identities are socially constructed, then it is important to ask how current relations of power affect those constructions, as well as whether and how such constructions might look different under more ideal conditions. And if identity is politically salient, as I have argued it is, then the construction of identity is an inherently political process. The discursive-democratic model of identity formation specifies an ideal relation between socially constructed identities and normative political structures: a relation of communicative freedom. It provides a link, in other words, between identity politics and concerns for social justice in general.

If such a theory is valuable, then it ought to be able to engage and clarify current debates about identity. In the following chapter, then, I will consider the debate concerning racial identity as a sort of test case. This debate provides a useful point of application since one of its central questions is whether a collective identity that has been constructed largely as a means of oppression can be reconstructed in a normatively justifiable way, or whether it must be abandoned altogether. It considers, in other words, the possibility of transforming an oppressive, ascriptive identity into a positive, self-ascribed identity, precisely the process that I have outlined in general philosophical terms in the pages above. Using the discursive-democratic model of identity construction as a guide, then, my aim is to determine whether racial identity would be justifiable under ideal, non-oppressive conditions. Let me now turn to this final task.

NOTES

1. Linda Alcoff, *Visible Identities: Race, Gender, and the Self* (Oxford: Oxford University Press, 2006): 22.
2. See Karl Marx, "On the Jewish Question," in *Collected Works*, vol. 3 (New York: International Publishers, 1975): 146-74.
3. Jürgen Habermas, "Technology and Science as Ideology," in *Toward a Rational Society: Student Protest, Science and Politics*. translated by Jeremy Shapiro (Boston: Beacon Press, 1970): 80-123.
4. Habermas, "Technology and Science as Ideology." 120.
5. Habermas, "Technology and Science as Ideology." 120.
6. Habermas, "Technology and Science as Ideology." 120.
7. Alcoff, *Visible Identities*. 15. The source of Alcoff's discussion and quotation, The Combahee River Collective's "A Black Feminist Statement," can be found in *Capitalist Patriarchy and the Case for Socialist Feminism*. edited by Zillah R. Eisenstein (New York: Monthly Review Press, 1979): 362-72.

8. Such "reforms" are exemplified by Grove City College v. Bell 465 U.S. 555 (1984) as well as Reagan's veto of the Civil Rights Restoration Act. For a more comprehensive view of the neoliberal assault on civil rights advances, see Nicholas Laham, *The Reagan Presidency and the Politics of Race* (Westport, CT: Praeger, 1998); and Gerald W. Heaney, "The Political Assault on Affirmative Action: Undermining 50 Years of Progress Toward Equality," in *Civil Rights and Race Relations in the Post Reagan-Bush Era*. edited by Sameul L. Myers (Westport, CT: Praeger, 1997): 217-27.

9. See my discussion of Habermas's analysis of feminism and other identity-based movements in chapter 2. The claim that cultural and ethnic minorities may not be transformative in the way that feminism was can be found in Taylor's *Multiculturalism*. 118.

10. See, for example, Arthur Schlesinger, *The Disuniting of America: Reflections on a Multicultural Society* (New York: Norton, 1992); David Hollinger, *Post-ethnic America: Beyond Multiculturalism* (New York: Harper Collins, 1995); and Todd Gitlin, "From Universality to Difference: Notes on the Fragmentation of the Idea of the Left," in *Social Theory and the Politics of Identity*. edited by Craig Calhoun, (Cambridge: Blackwell, 1994): 150-75.

11. See "What is a People: The Frankfurt 'Germanists' Assembly' of 1846 and the Self-Understanding of the Humanities in the *Vormarz*," in Habermas. *The Postnational Constellation*. 1-25.

12. Habermas, *The Inclusion of the Other*. 113.

13. Habermas, *The Inclusion of the Other*. 135.

14. Carl Schmitt, *The Concept of the Political*, translated by George Schwab (Chicago: University of Chicago Press, 1996).

15. Historically however, such a view of identity was not uncommon. Kant's *Anthropology from a Pragmatic Point of View* (Cambridge: Cambridge University Press, 2006), for example, attempts, through the "science" of anthropology, to "cognize the interior of the human being from the exterior," purporting to discover four racial types and linking them to differential intellectual and moral capabilities and personality characteristics. Similar attempts include Hegel's "Anthropology" in his *Encyclopedia of the Philosophical Sciences*, Johann Gottfried von Herder's *Ideas on the Philosophy of the History of Humankind*, and Arthur de Gobineau's *The Inequality of Human Races*. I will discuss these views in more detail in the following chapter.

16. In a critical but not unsympathetic attempt to sort out the complexities of "social constructionism," Ian Hacking begins *The Social Construction of What?* (Cambridge, MA: Harvard University Press, 2000), with a lengthy list of things which have been purported to be socially constructed, from "danger" and "emotions" to "youth homelessness" and "zulu nationalism." This list is meant to demonstrate just how variably the term "social construction" has been used, and how these uses have led to confusion about what, exactly, is being claimed. In what follows, I hope to avoid such ambiguity in regard to the social construction of identity, in part by modeling it after Habermas's description of discourse.

17. This is the interpretation of "constructivism" that Charles Mills prefers in "'But What Are You Really?' The Metaphysics of Race," in Mills, *Blackness Visible*. 47. David Ingram's *Rights, Democracy, and Fulfillment* also expresses this point nicely, noting that "conceding the 'socially constructed' nature of identities does not contradict the notion that such identities are largely imposed upon one by one's family, community, economic class, and culture." 17.

18. "Passing" is an interesting exception, but one that is clearly not available to all persons in racially categorized societies.

19. Habermas, *Between Facts and Norms*. 119-20.

20. These critics include contemporary contractarians as well who, like Rawls, attempt to provide a stronger "reasonable" foundation for political authority, without necessarily abandoning the individualism of traditional contract theory.

21. Lani Guinier and Gerald Torres, *The Miner's Canary: Enlisting Race, Resisting Power, Transforming Democracy* (Cambridge, MA: Harvard University Press, 2002): 11.

22. See my discussion of white identity in chapter 4.

23. Guinier and Torres, *The Miner's Canary*. 100.

24. See chapter 1.

25. John Rawls, *Justice as Fairness: A Restatement* (Cambridge: Harvard University Press, 2001): 4.

26. This doesn't mean that we shouldn't expect some of these problems to be *less prevalent* in ideal societies. For example, Rawls notes in *The Law of Peoples* (Cambridge, MA: Harvard University Press, 1999): 8-9, that in an ideally just world, the major causes of immigration—political and religious persecution, violations of human rights, and famine and extreme poverty—would disappear, and with them, the problems associated with immigration would disappear as well. The first claim—that the most problematic causes of immigration would at least be greatly mitigated if not eliminated—seems plausible enough. But it seems unrealistic to expect that such improvements would eliminate immigration entirely. That is, there may be still other reasons, good and bad, that persons choose to emigrate from their homelands and start lives in different places. So, although immigration might decrease drastically under ideal conditions, the necessity of managing the population, regulating borders, and so on might continue to raise not just bureaucratic issues, but issues of justice as well.

27. Rawls, *Law of Peoples*. 59-88.

28. Taylor, *Multiculturalism*. 133. At a lecture at Northwestern University in the fall of 2008, Habermas suggested that, insofar as members of such groups act in violation of these basic principles (presumably violating the law in the process), they should be treated as "normal criminals." I take this to mean that their actions need not be contextualized in terms of their collective identity or "comprehensive doctrine," in the way that legitimate exceptions to the law may be granted to other groups in multicultural societies.

29. Ingram, *Group Rights*. Ch. 4.

30. See, for example, Chantal Mouffe, *The Democratic Paradox* (London: Verso, 2000); Giorgio Agamben, *State of Exception*. translated by Kevin Attel (Chicago: University of Chicago Press, 2005); and *Homo Sacer: Sovereign Power and Bare Life*. translated by Daniel Heller-Roazen (Stanford: Stanford University Press, 1998).

31. Certainly, struggles against oppression often require a strategic attitude that is inappropriate within ideal discourse. For this reason, *retributive* identity politics is *not* fruitfully conceived on the model of the discourse ethic. It may nonetheless be subject to certain moral constraints, but it is not my intention to theorize those constraints here.

32. Amy Gutmann, *Identity in Democracy* (Princeton: Princeton University Press, 2003): 121.

33. Peter Dews, ed., *Autonomy and Solidarity: Interviews with Jürgen Habermas* (London: Verso Press, 1992): 250.

34. Jürgen Habermas, *Moral Consciousness and Communicative Action*. translated by Christian Lenhardt and Shierry Weber Nicholsen (Cambridge, MA: MIT Press, 1990): 202.

35. Habermas, *Inclusion of the Other*. 34.

36. This formulation of the rules of discourse comes from Habermas's "A Genealogical Analysis of the Cognitive Content of Morality." 44. Later formulations vary slightly, but this formulation suffices to bring out the parameters of the discourse ethic and new possibilities for its application. Also, I have taken the liberty of giving these rules shorthand names for ease of reference (the inclusiveness condition, and so on). Habermas does not provide such a lexicon.

37. As suggested above, this does not mean that identity formation is not influenced by "external" forces—that is, the way that the group is seen by others—but only that the authority of group members regarding the *explicit* (re)construction and (re)interpretation of their collective identity be recognized and respected. Analogously, one can recognize that individual choices about what type of life to pursue are significantly affected by influences outside of the individual—friends, family, custom, etc.—without denying that individuals should be free to choose what type of life to pursue.

38. This is a common plight for so-called "double minorities," but perhaps in this context it is better to speak of "doubly oppressed" persons: persons who are members of more than one oppressed group, or (another way of saying the same thing) persons who are oppressed by virtue of their membership in more than one oppressed group. The point that the *Martinez* case makes clear is that sometimes the remediation of one group's oppression involves the exacerbation of another group's oppression and, insofar as an individual's identity is not coextensive with any particular collective identity (and in fact usually encompasses aspects of several

collective identities), this "trade-off" can sometimes manifest itself in one and the same person. My suggestion is that the rules of discourse can provide some guidance as to how to resolve such situations, though they do not provide any a priori solutions.

39. Kymlicka, *Multicultural Citizenship.*

40. See Judith Resnick, "Dependent Sovereign: Indian Tribes, States, and the Federal Courts," *University of Chicago Law Review* 56 (1989): 675-86. Gutmann, (2003): 53 f33 discusses this essay in an endnote. Their reference is to the 1939 General Allotment Act, which, it is argued, encouraged the tribe to set a strict policy on intermarrying, where before there had been none. See also Ingram. *Group Rights.* 118-20.

41. The ideal itself, however, does not suggest any particular obligations we may have to enact the ideal. It does not, for example, suggest that we are justified in coercing certain groups to be a certain way, or in disparaging them. As suggested above, however, it may be action guiding in cases where one group's right to self-ascription conflicts with another.

42. Habermas, *The Theory of Communicative Action.*

43. Ranjoo Seodu Herr, "Cultural Claims and the Limits of Liberal Democracy" *Social Theory and Practice* 34, no. 1 (2008): 25-48.

44. Herr. "The Limits of Liberal Democracy." 37.

45. Taylor. *Multiculturalism.*

46. Taylor. *Multiculturalism.* 130.

47. Ingram. *Critical Theory and Philosophy.* 130.

48. K. Anthony Appiah and Amy Gutmann, *Color Conscious: The Political Morality of Race.* Princeton: Princeton University Press, 1996. I discuss Appiah's position on race and racial identity in more detail in the following chapter.

49. By "who they 'really' are," I mean according to their own estimation, or else to the socially dominant mode of determining group membership, for example, according to heredity. I do not mean to suggest that the identities in question are in any sense "real."

50. Nancy Fraser and Axel Honneth, *Redistribution or Recognition: A Political-Philosophical Exchange* (London: Verso, 2003). I do not mean to suggest that my understanding of oppression is identical to her understanding of misrecognition. For one, she does not premise misrecognition on group membership, but rather, understands it as the denial of *self*-recognition. Still, the phenomena she understands in terms of misrecognition overlap significantly enough with those that I understand in terms of oppression. More importantly, however, her claim that these phenomena are not reducible to issues of distributive justice (nor vice versa) is the one that I endorse here. The details of our disagreement will become clearer in the following pages.

51. Fraser and Honneth, *Redistribution or Recognition.* 63.

52. Fraser and Honneth, *Redistribution or Recognition.* 8.

53. Alcoff, *Visible Identities.* 30.

54. For example, the 1963 "March on Washington for Jobs and Freedom," at which Martin Luther King Jr. delivered his famous "I Have a Dream" speech, explicitly listed its goals as "meaningful civil rights laws, a massive federal works program, full and fair employment, decent housing, the right to vote, and adequate integrated education." Clearly, then, concerns of distribution—of jobs, income, housing, and education—played a central role in even the most mainstream elements of the movement.

55. I am skeptical that there are "purely" distributive injustices, but even if there were, it would not undermine the argument.

56. This is not to deny the importance of groups like Skinheads Against Racial Prejudice (SHARP), who actively struggle against the kind of white supremacist worldview that is constitutive of neo-Nazism and attempt to break the link between that worldview and a certain physical appearance (SHARPs are, to the average observer, virtually indistinguishable from their white supremacist counterparts). Still, though the roots of such groups can be traced back to many of the same sources, the group's express aim is not to internally reform neo-Nazi subculture so much as to destroy it. That is, though one might interpret such groups as attempting to redefine what it means to be a "skinhead," it is not the case that such a project involves redefining what it means to be a neo-Nazi, since such a worldview is thought to be beyond reform.

57. See William Zellner, *Countercultures: A Sociological Analysis*, (New York: St. Martin's Press, 1995).

58. See Timothy S. Brown, "Subcultures, Pop Music, and Politics: Skinheads and 'Nazi Rock' in England and Germany," *Journal of Social History* Fall, 2004.

59. This is the implicit force of those familiar statistics about inequalities in wealth—that the income of the top 1 percent of earners is equal to that of the remaining 99 percent and so on. One might not think that such inequalities were so reprehensible if the least well off were able to achieve a basic level of well-being and happiness.

60. In a related vein, poverty, especially in its global manifestations, has recently begun to receive long overdue philosophical attention. Philosophers like Peter Singer, Thomas Pogge, and others have theorized global poverty as a distributive injustice of the highest order and attempted, in different ways, to emphasize the strong moral duty of rich nations and their citizens to eradicate it. In light of the previous discussion, one might think that poverty represents a purely distributive injustice, having little to do with misrecognition. One might think, in other words, that extreme poverty would be unjust even if those who experience it (the "least well-off," to use Rawls's euphemism) did not include a disproportionate number of any one identity group. Even if this were the case, however, poverty would still retain elements of misrecognition, since "the poor" represents a stigmatized group in itself, apart from its constitutive membership. What I mean is that the poor are often seen as somehow deserving of their condition: lazy, depraved, criminal, and even satisfied with their lot (as is demonstrated by the feigned envy of those who "choose" to live off of public aid rather than "work for a living"). This is as true of domestic as global poverty. Purely distributive approaches to poverty will thus fail to recognize this ascriptive aspect of poverty, which explains why the poor might also be seen as oppressed rather than simply unfortunate.

Chapter Four

The Future of Racial Identity

A Test Case

Racial oppression represents one of the most normatively pressing injustices of our time. Racial (and other kinds of) oppression also represents a serious challenge to the dominant, culture-based conception of group identity and group rights, or so I have argued. It is this challenge—one which multicultural liberalism fails to meet—that motivates the attempt to develop an alternative framework for understanding group identity and group rights, a discursive framework based upon a (Habermasian) conception of intersubjectivity, and a right to self-ascription derived from that conception. Now such a framework must be put to the test: first, to show that it is better equipped to address the very omission that motivates its development (an easy enough task given the relative lack of attention paid to racial oppression in the dominant multicultural liberal approach, and one that, at any rate, has largely been argued for in the previous pages); but more importantly, to show that it can prevail even in the dominant approach's own terms, the terms of *ideal theory*. Recall that the dominant approach's primary justification for omitting oppressed groups and oppression-based theories of group rights refers to the superiority of ideal theory and depends upon the claim that such alternative theories are at best temporary and philosophically contingent; while its own approach represents a principled, noncontingent account of group rights understood as "inherent" in certain kinds of (cultural) group membership. Contrary to this claim, the discourse-theoretical explication of the right to self-ascription provided in the previous chapters is itself an ideal theory of a certain sort, one that is also "inherently" justified in reference to group membership in the most general terms, but one that accounts for and gives central place to "nonideal" concerns, especially oppression. In this chapter I will apply this theory to the particular case of racial identity, entering a contemporary debate that, to my mind, has yet to produce a satisfactory response to the question of the future of racial identity. The structure of the argument is as follows. I begin by providing an extremely brief history of the development of the concept of race and of racial classification, in order to make clear why many find the concept inherently linked to racism and racial oppression. Yet despite this history, and against Appiah and other racial eliminativists, I argue that racial identity *can* be discursively justified, and thus uncoupled from its ascriptive origins as a tool or aspect of racial oppression. I then discuss examples of what a discursively acceptable conception of racial identity might be like, as well as examples of discursively unacceptable conceptions.[1] I take it that the success of this argument will further demonstrate the value (both relative and inherent) of the theoretical framework developed in the previous pages.

RACE AND RACIAL OPPRESSION: ANOTHER "INTERNAL RELATION"?

If one judges a concept solely by its history and origins, then the concept of race would seem to be doomed from the start. This is because the idea of race as it first emerged in the seventeenth century was both scientifically false and ethically dubious, at least, according to today's standards of scientific and moral validity. Yet its importance in understanding the development of modern society is not understated by Francois Bernier, widely agreed to be the first to use the term "race" in his 1684 essay "A New Division of the Earth," when he says that the differences among races is "so remarkable that it may be properly made use of as the foundation for a new division of the earth."[2] Still, Bernier's reflections on race are largely conjectural, based on his own travels and observations of phenotypic differences among the peoples he encountered. And though he reflects extensively on the relative beauty of different races (at one point hypothesizing that "you do not find handsome women in the countries where the water is bad, or where the soil is not vigorous and fertile"),[3] he does not yet link these phenotypic differences to differences in intelligence and character, nor does he purport to give a scientific account of how races relate to the human species in general.

A scientific conception of race first emerged, as has only recently been brought into the light of philosophical scrutiny, with the great philosopher Kant (and also, to some extent, the great botanist Linnaeus).[4] The "discovery" of the type of human diversity that Bernier documents, along with the Enlightenment's fetishistic obsession with classification and taxonomy, produced intense debates as to the relation of race and races to the human species as a whole. In particular, the question of whether different races evolved (to use the term somewhat anachronistically) from the same "root genus" (monogenesis) or whether they evolved separately, from different and unrelated ancestors (polygenesis), was a matter of serious contention. Against proponents of polygenesis, Kant argued that all human beings came from a single line of descent, but that that line of descent was subject to variation due to the actualization of different "seeds" corresponding to "natural predispositions."[5] And though he thought that *all* such seeds were present (as potencies) in the earliest human beings, only one became irreversibly actualized in each race according to a variety of environmental contingencies (heat, humidity, diet, and so on). Kant thus posited four basic races, white Europeans, black Africans, red Huns (from which he supposed Native American peoples to have descended), and olive-yellow Hindus (including most of the Asian peoples known to Europe at that time), from which he thought all other racial variations could be derived.[6]

Even if this particular conception of race was controversial among European thinkers, the "natural predispositions" that Kant saw as corresponding to his four races were surely taken as intuitively unproblematic. That is, that the white European represented the closest living example of the "root genus" of all racial "deviations" was considered (by the Europeans themselves, of course) obvious, evidenced by Europe's possession of "the most fortunate combination of influences of both the cold and hot regions," that "the greatest riches of earth's creation are found in this region," and that "the human beings living in this region were already well-prepared to be transplanted into every other region of the earth."[7] By contrast, then, the "natural disposition" of the other races were supposed to exhibit varying degrees of deficiency, including in their ability to grasp and thus self-apply the moral law, with Asians coming closest to whites, despite their supposed difficulties with abstract concepts; Native Americans being furthest (he describes their "natural disposition" as a "half-extinguished life power"); and Africans falling somewhere in between, amenable at least to servitude.[8] As is apparent, then, Kant's theory of race is also and simultaneously a theory of *racial hierarchy*—that is, a theory of white supremacy. Of course, this would not have been a novel conclusion. One must imagine that the "fact" of white supremacy would have been, for white Europeans of that time, close to an unshakable intuition that any theory of race must account for just as much as it must account for questions about the genesis of different races. Yet it may be more surprising to the contemporary reader encountering this embarrassing and heretofore concealed connection—that, as Mills says, "modern moral theory and modern racial theory have the same father."[9]

Further, as much as Kant's idea of race rests on questionable (to say the least) ethical premises, it also rests on bad science. As one might guess, modern science has discovered nothing resembling the "seeds" that supposedly determine racial membership, nor have the peculiar hypotheses of Kant and his contemporaries regarding the causes of different skin colors, bone structures, and facial features borne any scientific fruit. In fact, even after the revolutionary scientific programs of Darwin and Mendel, the search for a scientific basis for race turned out to be in vain.[10] It is now widely accepted that no biological or genetic basis exists for the organization and classification of human beings into different races. So why then does the idea of race persist, both in everyday understanding and in a variety of academic contexts? The question is especially pertinent given the fact that "racialism," understood as the belief that there are different, discrete races of human beings, is, or at least has been historically, bound up with racism, understood as the belief that "races" can be organized hierarchically according to intelligence, character, or some other measure of value (a belief that, insofar as it organizes and rationalizes systematic harm to those groups it ascribes to "inferior" races, is constitutive of racial *oppression*).

A common-sense answer to this question is that, though race is not "real" in any deep scientific or metaphysical sense, it is still an important concept for understanding contemporary social reality, given that racial categories still structure the experiences of individuals and the functioning of institutions in "racialized" societies. One need not believe in God to understand the horrors of the Spanish Inquisition (or, to use Appiah's example, one need not believe in witches to understand the functioning of the concept of witchcraft in early colonial New England). One can continue to hold that such concepts have a *social* reality, even if one denies that they are real in the deeper senses above. In relation to race, such a position has come to be called *constructivism*.[11] Racial constructivists accept that race has no biological foundation, yet they argue that, as a result of human action and the widespread, consequential successes of false theories like those presented above, race has come to be inscribed in the institutions and practices of contemporary societies in ways that cannot be illuminated without recourse to some conception of race. Accordingly, they hold that race does have a *sociohistorical* reality, even if it cannot be linked to biologically significant "racial" differences.

One of the earliest attempts to elucidate a constructivist account of race is given by W. E. B. Du Bois, who notes that while races "perhaps transcend scientific definition, nevertheless, [they] are clearly defined to the eye of the Historian and Sociologist."[12] Du Bois thus suggests that a race is a "vast family of human beings, generally of common blood and language, always of common history, traditions and impulses, who are both voluntarily and involuntarily striving together for the accomplishment of certain more or less vividly conceived ideals of life."[13] Aside from the talk of "common blood," then, Du Bois' conception of race emphasizes the historical and derives from shared historical experience and a notion of shared "ideals of life." Such ideals, he thought, are racially specific, such that each race of humanity has its own unique contribution to make to human history and civilization in general, including the "Negro race," which he thought had "not as yet given to civilization the full spiritual message which they are capable of giving."[14] Thus Du Bois advocated for racial institutions like the American Negro Academy in hopes that they could assist in fulfilling such a historical task.

Du Bois's sociohistorical conception of race has become a focal point for contemporary debates about race and racial identity. Racial eliminativists argue that since the concept of race has no real referent (and moreover, since "race-thinking" is often morally problematic), it should be discarded altogether. Kwame Anthony Appiah, one of the most fervent proponents of racial eliminativism, argues succinctly that "there are no races. There is nothing in the world we can ask race to do for us"; in short, that race "refers to nothing in the world at all."[15] His earliest arguments to this end take the form of a critique of Du Bois's idea of race. In "The Uncompleted Argument: Du Bois and the Illusion of Race," Appiah carefully challenges Du Bois's definition of race, arguing that it ultimately relies on and presumes a scientific account of race, even though Du Bois himself recognized that such an account is implausible.[16] As Appiah points out, the talk of "family," "common blood," and even common "impulses" and "strivings" all presupposes a view of race as something that is biologically inheritable, that is, a (pseudo) scientific view. If there is any hope of replacing such an account with a sociohistorical one, it is to be found in the idea of shared history and traditions. Yet these criteria, Appiah thinks, turn out to be insufficient, as they lead to a certain circularity. "When we recognize two events as belonging to the history of one race," he says, "we have to have a criterion for membership in the race at those two times, independent of the participation of the members in the two events."[17] This criterion cannot be common history, since "we would have to be able to identify the group in order to identify *its* history."[18] In other words, common history in the most general sense is shared by all of humanity. But in order to identify a particular history, say, black history, one must *already* have some way of determining who is to count as black, and so whose history is going to count as black history. According to Appiah, this lack of foundations leads Du Bois to constantly fall back on the scientific conception of race, with all of its corresponding difficulties, not surprising since, for Appiah, there is no other foundation, as race itself is a meaningless concept. In Appiah's own words, "substituting a sociohistorical conception of race for the biological one . . . is simply to bury the biological conception below the surface, not to transcend it."[19]

This reading of Du Bois, and the corresponding rejection of even constructivist accounts of race, has given rise to serious debate. Paul Taylor, for example, challenges Appiah's claim that Du Bois's reliance on common history involves a vicious circularity. Such an objection, he thinks, only holds if "there is nothing to be said about this history except that it is The

History of The Race."[20] Yet, Taylor argues, there is a more plausible interpretation of "common history" than this. It may indeed be impossible to identify black history in a totalized sense, as the history that all and only black folks share, without first knowing who counts as black. Yet this does not preclude identifying certain "parallel experiences" of "concrete individuals" that "when relevantly similar enough, justify putting those who've lived them into the same category."[21] This understanding of common history, the essence of which is captured in Du Bois's claim that "the black man is a person who must ride Jim Crow in Georgia," avoids the problem of circularity.[22] In the terms that I have developed in the previous pages, one might say that the experience of *oppression* is the common history that links black folks together, since, after all, systemic racial oppression has never had a great deal of trouble identifying its victims.

Similarly, Lucius Outlaw criticizes Appiah's strategy of considering each of Du Bois's criteria for racial membership *individually*, instead of recognizing that, for Du Bois, race is a "cluster concept" determinable not by any single criteria, but by "several properties taken *dis*junctively," such that *any* one criteria is sufficient, but no one criteria is necessary.[23] To point out that such an approach is inadequate as a *definition* of race is, Outlaw thinks, to misunderstand Du Bois's project, to assume that he was in search of a concept of races as "natural kinds" or "heritable racial essences," as Appiah does. This project, Outlaw claims, "was *not* simply—or even primarily—an effort devoted to definition and taxonomy. Rather it was a decidedly *political* project," a project involving "prescribing norms for the social reconstruction of personal and social identities" and "rotating the axis" of a vertical cultural value system which placed the cultural achievements of white Europeans at the top and those of African descent at or near the bottom.[24]

Both of these criticisms see Appiah's approach to Du Bois's conception of race as inadequate and/or inappropriate to the subject. In emphasizing the political and pragmatic nature of the project (Du Bois was, after all, as Taylor points out, a committed pragmatist), both Taylor and Outlaw transform the question from whether the idea of race refers to anything "real" to whether the concept is *useful* for political praxis. Appiah seems to worry that the notion of race necessarily (or as it were, unnecessarily) limits the ability of persons to develop their own identities in a free and creative way (i.e., that they are essentially *ascriptive*). Further, he seems to think that the notion of race inhibits the social theorist's ability to achieve a "hermeneutical understanding" of groups and group identities, as opposed to a fixed and rigid account of human types. Yet these alternative readings of Du Bois suggest that intentionality is at the heart of the race concept—that race is "real" in the same way as money or holidays are: because we (at least some of us) have agreed to give meaning to the concept. If such meanings lack precise referential boundaries, it is because they are always contestable and often contested.

Du Bois's conception of race, then, must be seen as an attempt to contest the dominant conceptions of his time, which linked biological racial essences with hierarchical differences in moral, intellectual, and cultural capacity. Such a conception could still be challenged, though challenging it on metaphysical grounds misses the point, and Appiah seems at times to recognize this, as his metaphysical arguments often slip into moral and prudential argumentation.

In such practical discourses, however, eliminativism faces serious challenges, for if race truly doesn't exist, then how can race-based policies ever be justified? Eliminativism, in other words, easily lends itself to a certain kind of conservative "color-blind" social policy. Such an approach to social policy proceeds from the ostensibly admirable normative principle that one's race should not matter in determining one's life chances; that, to use Martin Luther King's often quoted (and often misinterpreted) words, one's opportunities and social position should be determined by the "content of one's character" rather than the color of one's skin. Today such a principle has the legitimating force of near consensus, even if its implications are the subject of serious disagreement. Yet, as is often missed by those who enlist Dr. King in their struggles against affirmative action and other perceived instances of "reverse racism," such a principle is *aspirational*. That such a dream might one day become reality does not mean that in the present, where race and racism *still do* affect the life chances of raced persons in profound ways, one can eliminate such inequalities by ignoring them, and even making of their mere mention a kind of social taboo, an always illegitimate use of the "race card." Such an approach to social justice serves to conceal and thus perpetuate already existing inequalities in the name of equality itself. That is, "color-blind" liberalism errs in a way similar to multicultural liberalism. It presumes that what ought to be—racial equality on the one hand, and voluntary group membership on the other—already is.[25]

In *Color Conscious*, Appiah purports to take constructivist criticisms as well as concerns for social policy seriously, returning to and refining his metaphysical arguments against race, but ultimately conceding that it may be wise to retain a conception of "racial identity" for political purposes. Here Appiah acknowledges that "race" (a term he renders in scare-quotes to consistently remind the reader of his metaphysical skepticism as to the existence its referent) is not only an ascriptive signifier, but that it is also central to non-ascriptive "identification," which he understands as "the process through which an individual intentionally shapes her projects—including her plans for her own life and her conception of the good—by reference to available labels, available identities."[26] He acknowledges, in other words, that despite their complicated history and relation to racist practices of classification and hierarchy, racial identities may nonetheless be important and valuable to the persons they purport to classify, thus resisting a view to which he nonetheless claims to be sympathetic, a "metaphysical" conception that "count[s] nothing as a racial essence unless it implie[s] a hierarchy among the races."[27] Rather, he allows room, as it were, for a "recreational" conception of racial identity that sees one's "race" as a part of, but not wholly or even largely determinate of, one's personal identity, similarly, he thinks, to the way that some Americans identify with their Irish or Italian heritage. Appiah thus recognizes that, at least at the level of conceptual abstraction, race and racism are not logically or conceptually connected, even if their empirical codevelopment suggests otherwise.[28]

Still, these concessions to constructivism do not amount to an abandonment of racial eliminativism. Eliminativists like Appiah may concede that racial identities are important in the short term, for challenging and resisting racism both in its structural manifestations and in its individual psychological effects, while still insisting, as Appiah does, that "we need to go on to the next necessary step, which is to ask whether the identities constructed in this way are ones we can all be happy with *in the longer run*."[29] He implies that racial identities would not be satisfactory in the long term (presumably meaning under more ideally just conditions), since they have a tendency to be "too tightly scripted" and to "go imperial," overshadowing and even being supposed to determine other aspects of one's personal identity. Yet this is the extent of his argument against racial identities under more just social conditions. Nowhere does he argue that racial identity *necessarily* leads to these undesirable consequences. His final word is only that the "fruitful imaginative work of constructing collective identities for a democratic nation" must "recognize both the centrality of difference within human identity and the fundamental moral unity of humanity."[30] A conception of racial identity that met these conditions would presumably be acceptable. In the next section then, I will present and defend a conception of racial identity that would meet such conditions, further specified in the terms I have outlined in the previous chapter. That is, I will defend a conception of racial identity that is discursively justifiable, and that proceeds from Outlaw's intuition, shared by many, that racial identities are important "even if, in the very next instant, racism and invidious ethnocentrism in every form and manifestation were to disappear forever."[31]

A DISCURSIVELY JUSTIFIABLE CONCEPTION OF RACIAL IDENTITY

Anyone who has attempted to discuss outside of the halls of academia the claim that race doesn't exist knows that the thesis is generally met with confusion and even hostility. This is true, in my experience, across the spectrum of racial identification. Blacks, whites, Latinos, and Asians object equally, even when they understand the arguments against biological or scientific conceptions of race. One might chalk this up to a deep, perhaps even unconscious need to justify and protect racial privileges on the one hand, and to an equally deep, internalized oppression on the other(s). One might think, more simply, that the majority of people, who have come to accept a certain folk understanding of race, are just wrong. Lots of people have been wrong about lots of things in the past, and the fact that many people believe something does not make it true. Yet beyond indoctrination, ignorance, or other pernicious reasons, the idea that people resist racial eliminativism because race is important to them at least deserves consideration. That is, if race and racism are logically separable, as even Appiah admits, then perhaps they are socially and politically separable as well.

As is apparent from his comments above, Outlaw is perhaps, among philosophers at least, the most serious proponent of such a project. In the introduction to his work *On Race and Philosophy*, he sets out to defend a conception of race as a "real, constitutive aspect of determinate populations of human beings," a conception he sees as a third way between deterministic, "scientific" conceptions that see race as a fixed biological essence and accounts (both eliminativist and constructivist) that see race as arbitrary, ideological, fictional, or otherwise unreal.[32] By contrast, Outlaw understands races as "social-natural kinds": groups defined in reference to *both* social-cultural and physical-biological characteristics, or more precisely, groups defined by physical-biological characteristics *as they are interpreted, contested, and given meaning* by different sociocultural groups in different historical periods. In short, the fact that the meaning and extension of race is variable and contested throughout history and into the present does not mean that it is arbitrary and meaning*less*. Rather, Outlaw proposes that races develop and evolve, "as do all things in the natural world, but in ways that are characteristically human."[33] And though he concedes that racism and racial oppression have significantly affected the currently dominant racial ontology, he nonetheless thinks it wise to entertain the possibility that more or less distinct racial groups might be "the result of bio-cultural group attachments and practices that are conducive to human survival and well-being, and hence must be understood, appreciated, and provided for in the principles and practices of . . . a liberal, democratic society."[34]

In other words, the biological evolution of human groups is itself conditioned by normative regulations—rules about mate selection, treatment of "outsiders," duties to our environments, and so on—in ways that, presumably, are not the case for other animals. The constitution of races is the result of such normative arrangements, and serves no less a purpose, Outlaw thinks, than the survival of the group. Race (or perhaps race-ing), then, is an inherently normative enterprise, even as it draws from and transforms our physical and biological "nature" in a reflexive manner. The crucial task for Outlaw is to show that such an enterprise need not result in the kinds of racism and "invidious ethnocentrism" that have tainted so much previous thinking about race and resulted in the kinds of oppressive institutions and practices that structure societies today; that is, that the constitution and preservation of races can be "guided by norms that we hope—and our best judgments lead us to believe—will help us to achieve stable, well-ordered, and just societies, norms bolstered by the combined best understandings available in all fields of knowledge that have to do with human beings and that are secured by democratically achieved consensus."[35]

I am hesitant to agree with Outlaw that racially defined human groups represent an evolutionary advantage for the human species, not least because, for all of his insistence on the importance of incorporating the insights of natural and human sciences, he cites very little empirical research to support this view. But perhaps this is excusable, since it is difficult to determine whether the conclusions of such research would hold under more ideal (nonracist) social conditions anyway. That is, there is no way to determine whether, for example, observable expressions and tendencies of solidarity among racial minorities are the result of some inherent commonality, or whether they are contingently effective means of combating racial prejudice. The problem is that there is no nonracist "control" society to establish the extent to which such conclusions are contingent upon current social conditions, where racism is still a relevant variable. This leads one to conclude, with David Ingram, that "even if it were true that cultural and physical similarities functioned as principle loci for group solidarities in the past, it is not necessary that they continue to do so in the future."[36] This is especially true given Outlaw's own emphasis on the way that sociocultural norms can transform "human nature" itself. One must imagine that such a dynamic anthropological adaptability would include (at least in principle) the ability to transcend even the kinds of bio-social groupings that Outlaw understands in racial terms.

Still, even if racial identification does not present clear evolutionary advantages, one might nonetheless grant the desirability, or at least, acceptability of a "voluntary separatism based on positive attraction of those who think, act, talk, and (yes) look alike . . . rather than on hatred of those who are different from oneself," as even a critic of Outlaw like Ingram does.[37] This line of investigation shifts the focus away from natural history and empirical fact and engages directly with those norms that "help us to achieve stable, well-ordered, and just societies," norms that are "secured by democratically achieved consensus." Such an approach is separate in principle from the question of whether racial identification is necessary, since one could hold a view of human nature (for example, one which sees humans as naturally selfish, sinful, evil, or murderous) in which highly undesirable and even immoral phenomena are nonetheless understood as natural and thus necessary.[38] In the previous chapter I argued that norms of discourse are helpful and appropriate for understanding collective identity formation and for circumscribing the limits of identity politics. As I mentioned there, there is a certain peculiarity about using universalizing procedural norms to illuminate the construction of particular collective identities. This peculiarity is brought into even sharper relief when placed within the concrete context of racial identity, since the very argument about "conserving" races is precisely about *maintaining* certain differences and appreciating the legitimacy (or, for Outlaw, inevitability) of certain kinds of *exclusion*. What would it mean, for example, to include everyone who could make a "relevant contribution" in discourses about racial identity? And to what, one might wonder, would they contribute? If one wants to use a discourse-theoretical approach to understand racial identities and their justifiability, one must clarify these complex issues.

The kind of exclusion at issue here is different from the (asymmetrical) tactical kind of exclusion that oppressed groups might demand based upon their oppression—the exclusion of men from all-woman groups, the formation of exclusive black or Latino organizations, and so on. That kind of exclusion or separatism is often justified based upon nonideal circumstances: imbalances of power that make oppressed groups vulnerable in ways that other groups are not, and therefore merit special protections that for other groups (men, whites, etc.) would be unjustified. Exclusion from (even ideal) discourse is a different matter. It does not derive from asymmetries of power, so much as considerations of relevance. My exclusion, for example, from discourses about the meaning of Polish-American identity need not be based upon the oppression of Polish-Americans but on the simple fact that I am not Polish, and so my contributions are not relevant. This kind of exclusion is not insidious, since it is based on rational considerations rather than power or coercion. Yet how, to return to the question at hand, does this kind of exclusion apply to discourses on *racial* identity in particular?

A strict defender of Du Bois could fairly straightforwardly interpret the inclusiveness condition by arguing that relevant contributions come from members of a particular race, defined by some combination of physical, cultural, and historical features, and that their contributions are contributions to the unique "message" of the race. Yet even if Du Bois's conception of race holds up to scrutiny, the idea that each race has a unique historical and even "spiritual" message is one that even defenders of Du Bois hesitate to endorse. To "conserve" races is one thing, but to advocate this kind of racial teleology seems to return to the problematic view that one can derive differences in character, ability, intelligence, and so on from racial differences. At any rate, the idea that individuals of the same race share some robust purpose or historical task does not mesh well with post-metaphysical approaches to normative justification and underestimates the diversity of perspectives among individual members of a particular race. In perhaps more familiar terms, it is false (and also not theoretically necessary) to presume that members of the same race share a strong conception of the good.[39]

Rather, "relevant contributions" could be interpreted as contributions to an ongoing project of interpreting the meaning of racial membership. Such a project begins (and has begun) with those who share a certain history of parallel experiences, as Taylor notes, but it need not exclude those who don't share those experiences or whose experiences are atypical. For example, the contributions of mixed-race persons have emphasized the inadequacy of a binary system of racial identification based on the illusion of racial purity. Perhaps the first to give sustained philosophical attention to the idea of mixed race, Naomi Zack shares Appiah's skepticism about the existence of races. In *Race and Mixed Race*, she provides similar arguments to show that race has no scientific foundation and further, that folk criteria of race, which attribute racial membership based primarily upon heredity, fail to achieve their purported goal of completeness (such that *all* persons would have a designated racial membership), since mixed-race persons do not fit within their classificatory scope.[40] Still, even though she denies that races are "real" in any important sense, she does consider the possibility of an acceptable, nonbinary system of racial identification. She asks her readers to imagine two races, P and Q:

> If the society in which P's and Q's lived were value-neutral about P and Q, then S and T, as mixtures of P and Q, might privately decide that they were both P and Q or that they were perhaps a different race, O. If racial designations were important for some reason (albeit still value-neutral), then individuals such as S might insist that the "authorities" recognize the existence of O. Alternatively, T's, who were more Q than P, might shrug and call themselves Q's. There might also be U's, the offspring of P-Q's and P's, who were more P than Q, and these U's might call themselves P's or insist on a new racial designation, N. At any rate, it would be possible, if society were neutral regarding P and Q, to speak of individuals who were mixed P and Q, and to leave it up to those individuals to support research into their own new racial characteristics and ultimately make a decision about how, as individuals of mixed race, they wished to be regarded racially. If racial categories were important for some reason, and if society were neutral about them and there were a fair degree of freedom and self-determination in that society, then that might be the dynamic of racial change.[41]

This passage nicely illustrates how the right to (racial) self-ascription is central to a normatively justifiable conception of racial identity. Zack's point is that "if racial categories [are] important," racially mixed persons (and insofar as the idea of racial purity is essentially a myth, we are all "mixed" to some degree) should be able to choose their racial identifications, either from existing options or by creating new collective identities. This requires that racial identities be open and inclusive to a degree, but it does not require that they include *everyone*, anymore than any kind of actually existing discourse must (or even could) include every living person as a participant. In short, racial groups need not (and cannot) include everyone in order to approximate the norm of inclusiveness. This is both a descriptive claim—that, as a matter of fact, not everyone sees themselves as having a stake in discourses about the meaning of being black, Asian, mixed-race and so on—as well as a normative claim—that the exclusion of certain views, such as those that would denigrate or disrespect group members, is legitimate. Again, the point here is that the relations of inclusion and exclusion that constitute the discursive entity are not, contrary to the views of Schmitt and his followers, arbitrary or coercive, but *rational*—that is, agreeable *in principle* to all. That is to say, the norm of inclusiveness derives from the universal importance of collective identity for human development, rather than the relative importance (relative, that is, to the dominant race) of maintaining dominance, which is the underlying principle of most previous schemes of racial classification such as the "one drop rule." My only worry about Zack's hypothetical description is that it seems to imply that racial identity is an individual and "private" matter, rather than a kind of "public meaning" as Guinier and Torres note (and as all collective identities are, as I argued in chapter 2). If this is in fact her meaning, then I fear the project of racial (re)construction that she describes may succumb to the kind of postmodern schizophrenia that Walzer convincingly criticizes.[42]

Similarly, Linda Alcoff draws from the history of Latin American racial identification, in which mixed race is the norm rather than the exception, to develop a positive reconstruction of mixed race or "mestizo" identity.[43] In the first place, this "new" racial designation is meant to account for the experiences of people who have no place in the dominant, biracial system of classification; to create a "linguistic, public, socially affirmed identity for mixed race persons."[44] Yet, it is also more than a mere addition to the available options for racial identification. Again, insofar as we are all racially mixed in one way or another, mestizo identity confronts the dominant idea of race, in which all persons have a distinct, nonoverlapping, hereditary racial identity with an alternative model valued for its "inclusivity and dynamism."[45] Mestizo identity is not just about giving a name to the nameless. It rather competes in the realm of racial discourse to encourage the already named to rethink their identity as well. Still, even though such a racial identity could, in principle, apply to everyone, Alcoff does not insist that it *must*. She preserves the possibility, in other words, that Q's could still "shrug and call themselves Q's." In accordance with the freedom condition of discourse,

Alcoff's conception of mestizo race encourages us to rethink our racial memberships, but it does not *coerce* us to do so. Mestizo racial identity, then, is a good example of a discursively justifiable conception of racial identity.

Having outlined a positive proposal, then, let me continue to clarify the application of discursive principles to the construction of racial identity by outlining a conception that I take it would not meet those conditions.

WHITE RACIAL IDENTITY

Is it the case, one might wonder, that whites, when confronted with a confusing array of diverse racial identities, might simply shrug and call themselves white? That is, could whiteness continue to exist as an option for racial identification, and, if not, what options does this leave for persons traditionally considered white? The question is an especially pressing one if collective identity is of constitutive importance in the ways that I have described, and since one might think that the lack of a positive reconstruction of white racial identity leaves a void that is too often filled by traditionally racist, white supremacist conceptions of whiteness. The answer, I believe, is that white identity is not discursively justifiable, mainly because it is inherently coercive and exclusionary, failing, at least, the first and fourth conditions of discourse. Yet, I will argue, this lack of justification need not cause too much worry, since white identity lacks the intersubjective resources and benefits of other kinds of collective identity, such that, in the absence of other, illegitimate kinds of benefits (i.e., all of the economic, political, psychological, and social benefits associated with being in a position of relative dominance) one wouldn't expect it to remain of much use to those it purported to describe anyway. That is, in precise opposition to the standard view that sees whiteness as the norm and nonwhiteness as the deviation or exception, I will argue that white identity is actually the anomalous identity, one that, when uncoupled from the system of racial oppression in which it formed, fails to provide the benefits typical of collective identity. If this is true, and if one accepts what I have called in the previous chapter the "democratic selection thesis," then one should expect that white identity would eventually be replaced by more useful and democratic forms of collective identification. The outlines of such alternatives are already visible even in our own society, and demonstrate that the illegitimacy of white racial identity does not leave white people "marooned" without any resources for collective identification.

In order to begin to understand why white racial identity is illegitimate, one must understand its history and the conditions under which it formed. Presumably, white racial identity stands in some relation to European heritage, though one should be cautious about equating the two. Previous to the eighteenth century, the idea of race as denoting specific lines of descent still marked a division between the "noble races" of European stock and their ignoble, though nonetheless similarly pigmented, countrymen.[46] At its most general, this idea of race allowed for a commonality among nations or peoples, circumscribing the membership of the French, German, or English "races." It was only in the New World, where English and other Europeans were confronted with the reality of slavery, that whiteness came to denote a commonality among Europeans of different types.[47] Putatively setting aside old and deeply ingrained internal inequalities, the express purpose of such an identity was to distinguish the free European from the enslaved African, based upon the latter's supposedly inherent dependency. In this way, slavery could be reconciled with the nascent values of liberalism. This opposition of slave and freeman is at the root of the United States' binary racial system, a system into which successive waves of immigrants would be forced to assimilate.

Such a collective identity, which depended upon the lack of discursive equality, coercion in a most concrete form, and systematic exclusion of "relevant contributions," would obviously not meet the discursive conditions for legitimating collective identity. On the face of it, however, this historical fact does not preclude the possibility of a positive reconstruction of white identity that recognizes the illegitimate origins of whiteness in order to replace them with new, more appropriate foundations. If black racial identity, which was born from the ignorant, hateful, and false ascriptions presented above, can be reconstructed and reinterpreted in a positive way, one might think, then, that white identity could be similarly transformed. This is a version of what Ingram calls the "symmetry thesis," the idea that "if it is legitimate for oppressed racial and ethnic minorities to affirm their respective racial and ethnic identities, then it must be legitimate for whites to do so as well."[48] Ingram rightly rejects such a thesis, on account of the fact that the many asymmetries of power that advantage whites over nonwhites provide strategic and political reasons for nonwhite racial solidarity, pride, and even "defensive" racism that do not exist for whites. Yet whether such an argument would still hold in contexts defined by more symmetrical relations of power (that is, by greater equality) among races is less than clear. One might think that under such conditions, where strategic concerns no longer provide compelling reasons for defensive racial solidarity, the appropriateness (or inappropriateness) of racial affirmation could be determined in a general way, a way that would apply equally to both whites and nonwhites.

To the contrary, I think that white identity can be shown to be illegitimate even under ideal political circumstances. The problem with whiteness is not, ultimately, that its substantive commitments are somehow immoral, undesirable, or vicious. Rather the problem, in this context, is that whiteness *lacks* any substantive foundation. There is no underlying value that can be retrieved, reinterpreted, or rediscovered when the unsavory exterior of privilege, power, and violence is stripped away. Whiteness is, at bottom, empty. Despite all of the positive characteristics that supposedly correspond to European culture—rationality, temperance, beauty, virtue, and so on—*whiteness*, as an identity meant to bind together diverse European cultures and distinguish them collectively from those Europeans meant to oppress, is a purely negative construction. It is defined, as the brief history of its birth above illustrates, by what it is *not*. Whites are not (and cannot be) slaves; whites are not savages; whites are not, above all, Africans. Likewise, and still today, one's whiteness is determined primarily by the *absence* of nonwhite ancestors, unlike nonwhiteness, which is determined, according to the one-drop rule, by the *presence* of (at least one) nonwhite ancestors. The complete lack of substance, and corresponding lack of verifiability of such a "unity based on an absence," is, strangely enough, illuminated by Zack's seemingly intentionally opaque representation of the essence of whiteness, which notes that "the sole determinant of A's whiteness is the absence of any individual who is defined by the presence of one individual who cannot be defined by the absence of those individuals whose absence defines A."[49] If this sounds like Hegelian logic, it is no coincidence. As black thinkers from Fanon to Du Bois have never failed to recognize, the modern binary racial system is a nearly literal instantiation of Hegel's master/slave dialectic. Though whites hold coercive power over nonwhites in a variety of ways (objective as well as subjective), white racial identity itself depends wholly upon the subjugation of its racial other for its existence. Without that power, the seemingly solid notion of whiteness melts into air. To state the conclusion simply: white racial identity depends upon and *only* exists within the context of white supremacy.

In concrete terms, this means that, despite its privileged status, white identity fails to provide for its members the resources typical of other collective identities. Insofar as certain presuppositions structure interaction and communication among whites (such as the presumption of white superiority, and the presumption that all whites unconditionally accept and defend the privileges of whiteness, and so on), it may be possible to speak of a *white lifeworld*. Such a lifeworld enjoys a social and political privilege which is reproduced through acceptance of its central presumptions. Nonetheless, it must be understood as culturally impoverished. This is because the privileges of whiteness are bought at the cost of the loss of the cultural, ethnic, and national identities from which whiteness recruits. In the United States, what is important above all is not one's Italian-ness, Irish-ness, and so on, but one's whiteness. Yet the latter does not provide resources for social integration, identity formation, and mutual understanding equivalent to the former. This is why, as Noel Ignatiev quips, "the typical 'white' American male spends his childhood as an Indian, his adolescence as an Afro-American, and only becomes white when he reaches the age of legal responsibility."[50] This desire for "crossover" (one might add the adolescent fetish for Zen Buddhism and other vaguely "eastern" ideas) attests to the inadequacy of white identity as a basis for relating to others on equal footing in increasingly diverse social settings.[51] Unlike other racial identities, which are perceived, rightly or wrongly, as having a certain content, whiteness is thought to lack content, such that, for example, often only nonwhites are described as "ethnic."[52] The result is that whiteness has come to be synonymous with "boring," "average," and "conformist," none of which are things that adolescents (who, after all, are engaged in the project of identity formation more directly than any other demographic) want to be.

Moreover, the background assumptions involved in affirming a white identity (and thus reproducing a white lifeworld) actually impede, rather than facilitate, communication oriented toward mutual understanding. As Mills notes, "part of what it means to be constructed as 'white' . . . is a cognitive model that precludes self-transparency and genuine understanding of social realities."[53] For example, most whites today seem genuinely puzzled about blacks' insistence on the reality of racial oppression, since they believe that everyone's life chances are determined primarily by effort and willingness to work hard. If certain groups fail to succeed, then it must be the result of a lack of such qualities, or a lack of the motivation to develop them. Such a view is consistent with the familiar statistics on racial inequality, as well as with the background assumption of white superiority, in this case, superiority of motivation, ingenuity, and industry. Similarly, whites in the not-so-distant past convinced themselves that nonwhites were not fully human, that they evolved from a different species, that some had tails and magical powers. Such false presumptions are the girders that support the white lifeworld, a lifeworld maintained by the exclusion of those who would dispute its false history and willful ignorance. In other words, white identity, like the Aryan racial identity of the Nazis, is founded upon an elaborate mythology that corresponds only tangentially to historical reality. Such a system of false beliefs replaces the "rational force of the better reasons" with coercive power. When that coercive power is abolished, those background assumptions are easily debunked, and the identity that they support collapses. The result is a lifeworld that is severely disabled in its public communicative competency. The various handbooks on "racial etiquette," "getting along with black people," and so on provide an illustration of this communicative disability that would be comical if its consequences were not so serious.[54]

So where does this leave young whites who want to distance themselves from the unjust advantages of whiteness and pursue more just social interactions? If collective identity is important, as I have suggested it is, not just for political action, but for human flourishing in general, then what identity can they claim as a basis for their own lives and their own political agendas?

Crossover and experimentation with nonwhite identities is one possibility, as indicated above. Yet one must proceed cautiously with such a suggestion, since crossover always runs the risk of expropriation, and since willingness to adopt the style, music, and "culture" of nonwhite peoples does not necessarily imply willingness to accept them as equals, let alone take up their struggles as one's own. Still, a cautious optimism about *sincere* crossover (let us not forget the third principle of discourse here) is part of the story about what "whites" are supposed to do with themselves in the wake of the abolition of whiteness. The other thing to note is that, although it may be unreasonable or unnecessary to presume that racial identity would disappear in an ideal society, it is not unreasonable to presume that it would be less important. Whereas in our society, Howard Winant observes, "to be without racial identity is to be in danger of having no identity," race might be less prevalent, if still important to some, in a more just society.[55] As Ingram notes, "in struggling against racism there are many positive nonracial identities whites can embrace—religious, secular humanist, and civic patriotic."[56] Also, one should not underestimate the value of art, sport, and other activities as a means of constructing a meaningful identity with others. Being involved with an underground music scene, an art collective, an organized sport like football or basketball, or a less organized sport like skateboarding can provide a sense of identity and community that provides resources similar to acceptable forms of racial identity, and can even, under the right circumstances, foster critical consciousness about the illegitimate identities that such communities replace.[57] Further, I see no reason to limit the scope or value of such collective identities to nonideal (retributive) identity politics. While they may be instrumentally valuable as a means for creating solidarity with other forms of antiracist identity politics, they are also valuable in themselves, as functional contexts for communication and socialization, and would be so even (or perhaps especially) under more ideal social circumstances.

Regarding the seemingly strange idea that some might have racial identities while others do not, I imagine there was a time when it seemed equally absurd for someone not to have a religious identity of some sort, even if it was "atheist" or "heretic." I imagine also that, for the people of that time, it would have been difficult to imagine religious identity as an object of choice, such that some people could choose none at all. Similarly, it is difficult for us to imagine a world in which some groups choose to define themselves racially, while others simply do not. But such a world is within the realm of the possible, and would be justified in reference to the discursive principles I have discussed in this chapter and the last. Therefore I think the worry about the lack of constructive alternatives for identity formation for white (or perhaps "formerly white") people is overstated. One must take care here, however, so that the situation does not become one in which only nonwhite people are considered "raced," while only (formerly) white people are considered raceless, a situation that would mimic the problematic normalization of whiteness that already exists today. Such a result does not, however, follow necessarily. The key is to assure that the right and ability to choose whether or not to identify oneself racially is equally available.

CULTURE RECONSIDERED

At the outset of this investigation, I criticized theories of group rights based upon the (instrumental) value of culture, largely because the intentionalist account of group membership that they presuppose fails, as a matter of social ontology, to account for the existence of non-intentional, oppressed groups, and therefore fails, as a matter of political morality, to provide a means for addressing the injustices experienced by such groups. Still, I noted there that, despite the failure of intentionalism as a descriptive starting point, intentionalism as an aspirational, normative goal is nonetheless defensible. That is, people *ought* to be able to freely choose their group associations and collective identities, even if, at present, large segments of society are not. One might wonder then, whether a normatively justifiable conception of race, one in which racial identities *are* freely chosen rather than ascribed, would have more in common with cultural groups than they presently do. Something like this intuition seems to be behind both theories, like Gould's theory of "intercultural democracy" discussed in the first chapter, that see culture as being more amenable to individual and collective interpretation ("more open and more fully free")[58] than conceptions of race, and so aim to replace conceptions of race with conceptions of culture, as well as theories, like that of Alain Locke and other founding members of the Harlem Renaissance, that aim to interpret race in cultural terms, without necessarily replacing it. In these final pages, I do not intend to develop my own conception of culture that could encompass the kinds of racial identity that I have argued would be acceptable under ideal discursive conditions, mostly because, as I have suggested throughout, I find the conception of culture too ambiguous and imprecise to be of very much use, beyond even the particular misuses it suffers at the hands of multicultural liberalism. Rather, I will conclude by arguing that even under ideal conditions, it would be unwise to think of races as cultures in the strong sense that multicultural liberals prescribe. This argument does not deny, however, that "culture," under some understanding of that term, might be a *part* of what it means to be a member of a racial group, as Du Bois's disjunctive conception of race suggests. Yet the extent to which one describes self-ascribed racial identities as "cultural" is largely a matter of semantics, and does not significantly alter the substance of the conception of self-ascription I have defended. Therefore I will limit myself to critical comments relating to the conception of culture specific to multicultural liberals like Kymlicka.

Though the explication of a normatively justifiable conception of racial identity that I have just undertaken occurs at the level of "ideal theory," it is wise not to forget the nonideal considerations that motivate it, especially insofar as these considerations shed light on the dangers of understanding race in cultural terms. I concluded the previous section with the claim that, under ideal conditions, the right and ability to choose whether and how to identify oneself racially should be equally recognized. One could say the same, I think, for culture, provided that one recognize that this is precisely *not* the case within the present system of racial ascription, in which the ability to self-ascribe one's cultural membership is *not* equally recognized. For example, imagine a white American with Irish, German, and Armenian heritage. Such an individual is free to choose whether and to what degree to identify herself with one, some, or all of these heritages, either superficially, say, through taking special interest in St. Patrick's Day festivities, or more seriously, by say, joining ethnic organizations, continuing or inaugurating ethnic traditions, and so on. Now imagine an "African American" (the term itself seems to limit at the outset the possibility of cultural self-ascription, and thus makes apparent the unequal distribution of such a possibility) with (of course) African, but also English and Irish heritage. Imagine, in fact, that he or she is not an African *American* at all, but English, or Irish. The cultural self-identification of such a person as English or Irish, beyond mere citizenship (which, to be sure, raises its own set of concerns), is likely to be met with a certain amount of confusion, especially in the context of American racial classification. Such a claim would likely lead, as Mills points out, to the further puzzling and ontologically confused question: "Yes, but what are you *really*?"[59] Compounding this inequality is the fact that the brutal reality of slavery has made it difficult if not impossible for most black folks to determine their heritage any more specifically than is given by the general term "African," thus denying them the richness of detail available to one who claims not European, but Italian, Greek, or Swedish heritage. Again, this must be understood in terms of inequalities in both the *opportunities* for cultural self-ascription, as well as the *social recognition* of those opportunities that do exist, and suggests that the greater freedom and openness of the concept of culture that Gould (and others) point to is itself a product of a certain kind of privilege.

Whether this would remain true in an ideally just society is less clear. In one sense, the extent to which race and culture might have a greater overlap under conditions of free self-ascription is outside the scope of philosophical speculation. That is, the extent to which a legitimate racial group understood itself in relation, for example, to a cultural understanding of the African diaspora could only be determined by that group themselves. That, again, is the very meaning of a right to self-ascription. Suffice it to say that nothing in the previous pages rules out that possibility. As I said, however, I will limit my concluding comments to the strong conception of culture at work in multicultural liberalism, and suggest that discursively justifiable conceptions of race would *not* fit that description. This is, in the first place, because the conception of culture as "societal" or as a "social imaginary" involves, on the one hand, a separate and more or less complete governmental and economic institutional structure, and on the other a one-to-one relation of the culture to systems of religious belief, language, knowledge, and practice. Of course, most racial groups today do not differ from one another to such an extreme degree, especially within a given territory. Even the most radical proponents of black cultural and/or political nationalism would have to acknowledge this fact, admitting that the desirability of separate institutional structures and even separate territories is motivated more by nonideal political concerns for resisting oppression than by an attempt to accommodate significant cultural differences.[60] On the other end of the spectrum, I see no reason to preclude, a priori, the possibility that racial groups could overlap the boundaries of otherwise extremely diverse "societal cultures." This, after all, is the sentiment behind theories of diaspora, which posit an important commonality among groups that may have very different languages, customs, institutions, and practices, a commonality that cannot be simply reduced to an interest in combating oppression, or some other nonideal concern.[61]

To state the matter more precisely, the objection I mean to refute is one that would deny at the outset Kymlicka's claim about the "unusual" status of black Americans as neither national minorities nor ethnic groups. Rather, one might assert that black Americans do in fact possess a "societal culture," present in the practices and institutions of impoverished inner-city ghettos, and so should in fact be considered national minorities.[62] Or one might claim, as certain strands of black nationalism have, that the United States ought to recognize the social, political, and economic autonomy of black urban centers, a claim that also presupposes a kind of black societal culture, though as a solution (or at least a strategic necessity) rather than a problem to be overcome.

It is undeniable that racialized urban ghettos do possess a kind of autonomy not present in other sectors of society, both in the troubling way that exclusion, segregation, and oppression force one to fend for oneself, and in the more promising way that such systematic injustices tend to produce practices and forms of solidarity that may be inherently desirable in spite of the undesirable conditions from which they arise. Yet both of the above sorts of views underestimate the extent to which such communities remain bound up with the larger society and "culture" in general. One can see this, for example, in the history of black music which, far from being autonomous, can only be understood in relation to the social and political contexts from which it arose, and which, reciprocally, is essential to any understanding of "American" music as a whole. Economically as well, the urban ghettos play a crucial role in the larger economic system: as pools for cheap, menial labor, but also as carefully supervised and controlled reservoirs for structurally necessary unemployment, as well as nearly unrestricted markets for deficient and even harmful goods.[63] In other words, the lack of a distinct African American societal culture must be understood in part as a result of black exploitation, which is in fact a certain kind of integration, though not one that leaves any room for autonomy or self-ascription.

That is to say, I think Kymlicka is right to note that black Americans fit neither the mold of the national minority, nor that of the ethnic group, though I take issue with the conclusions he draws from this claim. The idea of a "societal culture," possession of which is a necessary condition for being considered a national minority, does little to clarify the situation of black Americans, or of blacks in general, as in those descended from Africa but populating nearly all nations, societies, and cultures of the world. Under current conditions, however, it is understandable that political theorists would find value in the task of theorizing foundations for black political solidarity, and "culture," in one sense or another, has long played a part in that project. Yet the political project of resisting oppression must be distinguished from the creation and development of cultural lifeworlds, and the latter should not be seen as a requirement for the former. In *We Who Are Dark: The Philosophical Foundations of Black Solidarity*, Tommie Shelby makes precisely this point, against those who believe that black solidarity must include a commitment to black cultural autonomy.[64] Shelby identifies eight "tenets of black cultural nationalism":

1. Distinctiveness: There is a distinct black culture that is different from . . . white culture.
2. Collective Consciousness: Blacks must rediscover and collectively reclaim their culture, developing a consciousness . . . rooted in this heritage.
3. Conservation: Black culture is an invaluable collective good that blacks should identify with.
4. Rootedness: Unlike white culture, black culture provides a stable and rich basis for . . . the construction of positive and healthy individual identities.
5. Emancipatory Tool: Black culture is an essential tool of liberation, a necessary weapon to resist white domination.
6. Public Recognition: The state should refrain from actions that prevent the endogenous reproduction of black culture.

7. Commercial Rights: Blacks must become the primary producers, purveyors, and beneficiaries . . . of their culture.
8. Interpretive Authority: Blacks are . . . and should be regarded as the foremost interpreters of the meaning of their cultural ways.[65]

Of course, all of these claims rise or fall with 1, which I have argued is false if one means by culture "societal culture" as Kymlicka understands it. Yet Shelby leaves the meaning of culture open here, giving the benefit of the doubt to those who might specify it in a more plausible way. And as I mentioned above, nothing in the previous pages suggests that the kind of collective identity arrived at through processes of self-ascription could not be "cultural" in some slightly weaker sense than Kymlicka's. So, I will follow Shelby and grant this claim, if only for the sake of argument.

I am sympathetic to most of the other claims as well. I explicitly defended 4 in the previous section, and 6 and 8 are both, in different respects, related to what I have called "self-ascription." 5 is a decidedly nonideal claim, one which is also probably true, but separable from the inquiry at hand; and 7 is also beyond the scope of this analysis, having to do with the formal structures of the economy, of which I am not explicitly concerned here. Let me focus, then, on 2 and 3, which are quite similar, and in particular on the nature of the normative prescriptions presented there (blacks *must* develop a collective consciousness, blacks *should* identify with and conserve their culture). As Shelby points out, there is a fundamental difference between the claim that blacks (or for that matter any group) should be *allowed* to develop and maintain a racial and/or cultural identity, and the claim that blacks (or any other group) are *obligated* to develop and maintain such an identity. The right to self-ascription implies the former but not the latter. As Shelby notes, "it is perfectly consistent with such a right or goal [the right, as he has it, to "be free to develop and maintain their cultural identities without being inhibited by unjust measures or artificial barriers"] that those blacks who do not desire this form of group self-determination are free to cultivate an alternative cultural identity, even to assimilate completely to white culture."[66] Yet 2 and 3 do seem to allow for this possibility, entailing as they do the stronger claim that blacks are obligated to identify with, support, and conserve black culture. I agree that this claim is mistaken, such that one should not expect or require that all persons now classified as racially black would self-ascribe as racially or culturally black under conditions of free self-ascription. Thus this chapter argues for the *possibility* of legitimate racial identification but not for the *necessity* of racial identification.

Still, when Shelby concludes from all this that black solidarity does not require a shared collective identity, he seems to have in mind the stronger type of collective identity that Habermas names "ethical-cultural" identity.[67] He does not seem to consider the distinction that I outlined in the second chapter, between this kind of collective identity and a weaker, "ethical-political" collective identity. Insofar as, as I argued there, practical political discourses (such as discourses on racial justice) presuppose and include discourses of collective self-clarification, the kind of solidarity he has in mind does in fact entail a weaker kind of collective identity, even if it is only the dynamic, ever-changing collective identity of interlocuters engaged in such discourses rather than enduring racial and/or cultural identities. In other words, as I have argued in the previous chapters, the strategic struggle against oppression as well as the ideally functioning processes of democratic politics both presuppose and require certain kinds of collective identity, the former taking the creation of healthy collective identities as part of its strategic political task, and the latter having the luxury of taking them for granted. But the concept of culture, again, does little to clarify these collective identities or the processes by which they develop. This is true of collective identity in general and racial identity in specific. Thus the analysis of racial identity presented in this chapter provides further support for the critique of multicultural liberalism given in the first chapter, and gives a concrete example of the kind of self-ascription-based identity politics that can be justified in discourse-theoretic terms.

At this final juncture, then, I invite the reader to contrast the framework I have presented in this and the previous chapters with Kymlicka's own approach, as per his suggestion, based upon "our" moral ideals, which include, for me as much as for him, freedom, though not, I have suggested, in the problematic and unnecessarily limited sense of *individual* freedom, and equality, of which oppression makes a mockery. Another way one might compare these two approaches is in terms of their respective methodologies; not just in terms of a kind of individualism contrasted with a kind of intersubjectivism, but also in (not unrelated) terms of the perspective of the observer versus the perspective of the participant. The perspective of the observer sets out in advance the characteristics of a particular kind of group, say, a culture, or more specifically, a national minority, an ethnic group, and so on, by way of abstracting and generalizing from certain kinds of existing groups. Somewhat ironically, given the reliance upon ideal theory as a justification for the exclusion of certain kinds of groups, this approach makes it difficult to imagine how group affiliations and collective identifications might undergo fundamental changes, for example, from ascriptive to non-ascriptive, or vice versa, and how such changes bear upon more general social processes like democracy. By contrast, the participant perspective leaves the work of determining the nature of group associations, cultural or otherwise, to the members of those groups themselves, focusing instead on the conditions (both procedural and substantive) that would facilitate this process. This is why the right to self-ascription can be conceived without recourse to a conception of culture, and why the parameters of a democratic identity politics can be put forth without having to link such a politics to any identities *in particular*.

If the contrast is made in this way, I hope that the reader will conclude at least that there is more at stake in such a comparison than a shift of focus from ideal to nonideal theory. Rather, the approach that I have developed, while paying closer attention to and in a sense beginning from concrete concerns of nonideal theory, nonetheless suggests its own kind of procedural ideal, which differs in important ways from that of Kymlicka and other multicultural liberals, as this final chapter demonstrates. I hope that the reader will conclude further that the inability of multicultural liberalism to deal with the issue of oppression in general, and racial oppression in particular, marks, in light of "our" liberal values, an unacceptable failure, and that the account that I have developed is, in that regard, superior.

NOTES

1. By "acceptable" and "unacceptable" here, I mean by reference to the principles of discourse as adapted and applied to the construction of collective identity (see chapter 3). One could thus, if one wished, replace "acceptable" with "procedurally legitimate." The main feature that makes a racial identity "procedurally legitimate" is that it is self-ascribed, though there are other related procedural criteria as well, as shall soon become apparent.

2. Francois Bernier, "A New Division of the Earth," pp. 1-4, in *The Idea of Race*. edited by Robert Bernasconi and Tommy Lott (Indianapolis: Hackett, 2000): 1.

3. *The Idea of Race*. 4.

4. Kant's racial theory and the central role that it plays in his philosophical system has been presented most clearly by Emmanuel Eze's "The Color of Reason: The Idea of 'Race' in Kant's Anthropology," in *Anthropology and the German Enlightenment*. edited by Katherine Faull (Lewisburg, PA: Bucknell University Press, 1995): 196-237. Kant's conception of race suffices to demonstrate the link between scientific conceptions of race and the kind of racial hierarchies that we would now call racist, so I will limit my discussion to his account.

5. Immanuel Kant, "Of the Different Human Races," in *The Idea of Race*. 8-22.

6. Kant, "Of the Different Human Races."

7. Kant, "Of the Different Human Races" 19-20.

8. Kant, "Of the Different Human Races." See also Mills. *The Racial Contract*: 71.

9. Mills, *The Racial Contract*: 72.

10. Naomi Zack, *Philosophy of Science and Race*. New York: Routledge, 2002.

11. I discuss social constructivism about identity in general terms in chapter 3. For an account of the varieties of racial constructivism in particular, see R. Mallon, "A Field Guide to Social Construction," *Philosophy Compass* 2, no. 1 (2007): 93-108.

12. W. E. B. Du Bois, *The Conservation of Races* (New York: Forgotten Books: 2008): 4.

13. Du Bois, *The Conservation of Races*.

14. Du Bois, *The Conservation of Races*. 7.

15. Kwame Anthony Appiah, *In My Father's House: Africa in the Philosophy of Culture* (Oxford: Oxford university Press, 1992): 45.

16. Kwame Anthony Appiah, "The Uncompleted Argument: Du Bois and the Illusion of Race" in *Race, Writing and Difference*. edited by Henry Louis Gates (Chicago, University of Chicago Press, 1986): 21-37.

17. Appiah, "The Illusion of Race." 27.

18. Appiah, "The Illusion of Race." Original emphasis.
19. Appiah, "The Illusion of Race." 34.
20. Paul Taylor, "Appiah's Uncompleted Argument: Du Bois and the Reality of Race," *Social Theory and Practice*, 26 no. 1 (2000): 108.
21. Taylor, "Appiah's Uncompleted Argument."
22. W. E. B. Du Bois, *Dusk of Dawn* (New Brunswick: Transaction Press, 1984): 117.
23. Lucius Outlaw, *Critical Social Theory in the Interests of Black Folks* (Oxford: Rowman & Littlefield, 2005): 152.
24. Outlaw, *Critical Social Theory*. 153.
25. For more detailed criticisms of the color-blind approach, its justifications, and its effects, see Amy Gutmann's contributions in K. Anthony Appiah and Amy Gutmann, *Color Conscious: The Political Morality of Race* (Princeton, NJ: Princeton University Press, 1996); and David Caroll Cochran, *The Color of Freedom: Race and Contemporary American Liberalism* (Albany: SUNY Press, 1999).
26. Appiah and Gutmann, *Color Conscious*. 78.
27. Appiah and Gutmann, *Color Conscious*. 82.
28. Appiah and Gutmann, *Color Conscious*. 82.
29. Appiah and Gutmann, *Color Conscious*. 99. My emphasis.
30. Appiah and Gutmann, *Color Conscious*. 105.
31. Outlaw, *Critical Social Theory*. 159.
32. Lucius Outlaw, *On Race and Philosophy* (New York: Routledge, 1996): 2.
33. Outlaw, *On Race and Philosophy*. 11.
34. Outlaw, *On Race and Philosophy*. 12.
35. Outlaw, *On Race and Philosophy*. 2.
36. David Ingram, "Toward a Cleaner White(ness): New Racial Identities," *Philosophical Forum* 36 no. 3 (2005): 256.
37. Ingram, "Toward a Cleaner White(ness)." 277.
38. This does not mean that the expression of such undesirable phenomena cannot be restrained or controlled by convention. Traditional contractarians like Hobbes illustrate this point nicely, since their conception of human nature is rather negative and leads to undesirable results for human life, such that our rapacious "nature" must come under the rational control sovereign power.
39. Perhaps one could say that *oppressed* persons share an interest in eliminating their oppression, but this interest would presumably no longer bind these persons together once racial oppression is eliminated.
40. Naomi Zack, *Race and Mixed Race* (Philadelphia: Temple University Press, 1993).
41. Zack, *Race and Mixed Race*. 74.
42. See my discussion of Walzer's "On Involuntary Association" in chapter 1.
43. Linda Alcoff, "Mestizo Identity" in *American Mixed Race: The Culture of Microdiversity*. edited by Naomi Zack (Lanham, MD: Rowman & Littlefield, 1995).
44. Alcoff, *Visible Identities*. 282.
45. In developing this model, Alcoff draws from Mexican philosopher Jose Vasconcelos' idea of "*la raza cosmica*," the "cosmic race," which she describes as a theory of racial "inclusivity." See Jose Vasconcelos, *The Cosmic Race, La raza Cosmica: A Bilingual Edition*. translated by Didier T. Jaen (Baltimore: Johns Hopkins University Press, 1979).
46. George M. Fredrickson, *Racism: A Short History* (Princeton: Princeton University Press, 2003): 53-4.
47. Fredrickson, *Racism*. See also Noel Ignatiev, *How the Irish Became White.* (New York: Routledge, 1995). This doesn't mean that Europeans were previously unaware of their collective lightness in relation to darker Africans, but only that that difference had never before become so pronounced as to trump all others.
48. Ingram, *Rights, Democracy, and Fulfillment*. 65.
49. Zack, *Race and Mixed Race*. 28.
50. "Interview," in *Race Traitor*. edited by Noel Ignatiev and John Garvey (New York: Routledge, 1996): 289. Ignatiev and Garvey coedited the journal *Race Traitor*, the most important articles of which this volume anthologizes.

51. A recent headline in the satirical newspaper *The Onion*, reading "Asian Teen Gets Way into Western Philosophy," humorously reverses the white, Western desire for crossover. Perhaps an even more widespread testament to the poverty of white identity is the claim made by many whites, unburdened by any evidence, to have Native American heritage.

52. This contemporary sense of whiteness too continues to be expressed negatively, through a lack of certain qualities or abilities, such that not being able to dance, for example, attests to one's whiteness.

53. Mills, *The Racial Contract*. 18.

54. See, for example, Sheila Rush and Chris Clark's *How to Get Along with Black People: A Handbook for White Folks and Some Black Folks Too!* (New York: Third Press, 1971); and more recently, Nick Adams's *Making Friends with Black People*. (New York: Kensington, 2006).

55. Howard Winant, *Racial Conditions* (Minneapolis: University of Minnesota Press, 1994): 16.

56. Ingram, "Toward a Cleaner White(ness)." 263.

57. Skateboarding, for example, began as a mostly white sport, a derivation from surfing, but has now developed a distinctly urban style and has come to be truly multiracial. Punk rock, again mostly white, though it drew from Caribbean influences, has helped many white youths to develop critical consciousness about issues of class, race, gender, and so on as well as provided an outlet to explore and express this newly discovered consciousness.

58. Gould, *Globalizing Democracy*. 110.

59. See again Mills's essay by the same name in *Blackness Visible*.

60. To be clear, I am referring here to the specific tradition of black nationalism in the United States, and not to other varieties of nationalism, which may very well be based on an attempt to accommodate significant cultural differences. Even within this specific context, however, there are separatist views that would deny the claim, namely the kinds of separatism that still purport to link culture to race in a biologically reductive and deterministic fashion. I have in mind, however, the nondeterministic varieties of separatism that recognize that culture is not determined by race, which are, to my mind, the only varieties of separatism worth taking seriously.

61. See, for example, Paul Gilroy, *The Black Atlantic: Modernity and Double Consciousness*. (Cambridge, MA: Harvard University Press, 1993).

62. Sociologist William Julius Wilson defends such a view in *Social Justice in a Diverse Society* (Mountain View, CA: Mayfield, 1996). Ingram discusses his position in *Group Rights*. 81-85.

63. On the structural necessity of unemployment in capitalist societies, see David Schweickart, *Against Capitalism* (Lanham, MD: Rowman & Littlefield: 2002).

64. Tommie Shelby, *We Who Are Dark: The Philosophical Foundations of Black Solidarity* (Cambridge, MA: Harvard University Press, 2005).

65. Shelby, *We Who Are Dark*. 163-67.

66. Shelby, *We Who Are Dark*. 168.

67. Shelby, *We Who Are Dark*. 170.

Bibliography

Adorno, Theodor, and Max Horkheimer. *Dialectic of Enlightenment: Philosophical Fragments*. Edited by Gunzelin Schmid Noerr. translated by Edmund Jephcott. Stanford: Stanford University Press, 2002.
Agamben, Giorgio. *Homo Sacer: Sovereign Power and Bare Life*. translated by Daniel Heller-Roazen. Stanford: Stanford University Press, 1998.
———. *State of Exception*. translated by Kevin Attel. Chicago: University of Chicago Press, 2005.
Alcoff, Linda. *Visible Identities: Race, Gender, and the Self*. Oxford: Oxford University Press, 2006.
———. "Toward a Phenomenology of Racial Embodiment," *Radical Philosophy* 95 May/June 1998.
Appiah, K. Anthony. "The Uncompleted Argument: Du Bois and the Illusion of Race" in *Race, Writing and Difference*. Edited by Henry Louis Gates. Chicago, University of Chicago Press, 1986.
———. *In My Father's House: Africa in the Philosophy of Culture*. Oxford: Oxford university Press, 1992.
Appiah, K. Anthony, and Amy Gutmann. *Color Conscious: The Political Morality of Race*. Princeton, NJ: Princeton University Press, 1996.
Bernier, Francois. "A New Division of the Earth," in *The Idea of Race*. Edited by Robert Bernasconi and Tommy Lott. Indianapolis: Hackett, 2000: 1-4.
Chambers, Simone. "Can Procedural Democracy Be Radical?," in *The Political*. Edited by David Ingram. Malden, MA: Blackwell Publishers, 2002: 168-88.
Cochran, David Caroll. *The Color of Freedom: Race and Contemporary American Liberalism*. Albany: SUNY Press, 1999.
Cudd, Ann. *Analyzing Oppression*. Oxford: Oxford University Press, 2006.
Delaney, Martin. *The Condition, Elevation, Emigration, and Destiny of the Colored People of the United States*. New York: Ayer Company, 1988.
Dews, Peter ed. *Autonomy and Solidarity: Interviews with Jürgen Habermas*. London: Verso Press, 1992.
Doppelt, Gerald. "Is There a Multicultural Liberalism?" *Inquiry* 41 (1998): 223-46.
———. "Illiberal Cultures and Group Rights" *Journal of Contemporary Legal Issues* 12 (2002): 661-92
Douglass, Frederick. "The Folly of Colonization," in *African American Social and Political Thought 1850-1920*. Edited by H. Brotz. Transaction Publishers, 1992.

Eze, Emmanuel. "The Color of Reason: The Idea of 'Race' in Kant's Anthropology" in *Anthropology and the German Enlightenment*. Edited by Katherine Faull. Lewisburg, PA: Bucknell University Press, 1995: 196-237.

Fraser, Nancy. "What's Critical about Critical Theory? The Case of Habermas and Gender," in *Feminism as Critique: On the Politics of Gender*. Edited by Seyla Benhabib and Drucilla Cornell. Minneapolis: University of Minnesota Press, 1987: 31-56.

———. "Struggle over Needs: Outline of a Socialist-Feminist Critical Theory of Late-Capitalist Political Culture," in *Unruly Practices: Power, Discourse, and Gender in Contemporary Social Theory*. Minneapolis: University of Minnesota Press, 1989: 109-42.

———."Rethinking the Public Sphere: A Contribution to the Critique of Actually Existing Democracy," in *Habermas and the Public Sphere*. Edited by Craig Calhoun Cambridge, MA: MIT Press, 1992: 109-42.

Fraser, Nancy, and Axel Honneth. *Redistribution or Recognition: A Political-Philosophical Exchange*. London: Verso Press, 2003.

Frye, Marilyn. *The Politics of Reality: Essays in Feminist Theory*. Berkeley, CA: Crossing Press, 1983.

Garcia, Jorge. "The Heart of Racism," *Journal of Social Philosophy* 27 (1996): 5-45.

Gilroy, Paul. *The Black Atlantic: Modernity and Double Consciousness*. Cambridge: Harvard University Press, 1993.

Gould, Carol. *Marx's Social Ontology*. Cambridge: MIT Press, 1978.

———. *Globalizing Democracy and Human Rights*. Cambridge: Cambridge University Press, 2004.

Guinier, Lani. *Tyranny of the Majority: Fundamental Fairness in Representative Democracy*. New York: Free Press, 1994.

Guinier, Lani, and Gerald Torres. *The Miner's Canary: Enlisting Race, Resisting Power, Transforming Democracy*. Cambridge: Harvard University Press, 2002.

Gutmann, Amy. *Identity in Democracy*. Princeton, NJ: Princeton University Press, 2003.

Habermas, Jürgen. "Technology and Science as Ideology" in *Toward a Rational Society: Student Protest, Science and Politics*, translated by Jeremy Shapiro. Boston: Beacon Press, 1970: 80-123.

———. *Legitimation Crisis*. translated by Thomas McCarthy. Boston: Beacon Press, 1973.

———. *The Theory of Communicative Action. Vol. 2. Lifeworld and System: A Critique of Functionalist Reason*. translated by Thomas McCarthy. Boston: Beacon Press, 1981.

———. "An Alternative Way Out of the Philosophy of the Subject: Communicative versus Subject Centered Reason" in *The Philosophical Discourse of Modernity: Twelve Lectures*. translated by Frederick Lawrence. Cambridge, MA: MIT Press, 1987: 294-327.

———. *The Structural Transformation of the Public Sphere*. translated by Thomas Burger. Cambridge, MA: MIT Press, 1989.

———. *Moral Consciousness and Communicative Action*. translated by Christian Lenhardt and Shierry Weber Nicholsen. Cambridge, MA: MIT Press, 1990.

———. *Between Facts and Norms: Contributions to a Discourse Theory of Law and Democracy*. translated by William Rehg. Cambridge, MA: MIT Press, 1996.

———. "A Genealogical Analysis of the Cognitive Content of Morality" in *The Inclusion of the Other: Studies in Political Theory*. Edited by Ciaran Cronin and Pablo De Greiff. Cambridge, MA: MIT Press, 1999: 3-46.

———. "Remarks on Legitimation through Human Rights," In *The Postnational Constellation: Political Essays*. translated by Max Pensky. Cambridge, MA: MIT Press, 2001.

———. "Equal Treatment of Cultures and the Limits of Postmodern Liberalism," *The Journal of Political Philosophy* 13, no. 1 (2005): 1-28.

Hacking, Ian. *The Social Construction of What?* Cambridge: Harvard University Press, 2000.

Haslanger, Sally. "Oppressions: Racial and Other." In *Racism in Mind*. Edited by Michael P. Levine and Tamas Pataki. Ithaca: Cornell University Press, 2004: 97-123.

Herr, Ranjoo Seodu. "Liberal Multiculturalism: An Oxymoron?" *The Philosophical Forum*, 38, no. 1 (2007): 23-41.

———. "Cultural Claims and the Limits of Liberal Democracy," *Social Theory and Practice*, 34, no. 1 (2008): 25-48.

Honneth, Axel. *The Struggle for Recognition: The Moral Grammar of Social Conflicts.* translated by Joel Anderson. Cambridge: Polity Press, 1995.
———. *Disrespect: The Normative Foundations of Critical Theory.* translated by Joseph Ganahl. Cambridge: Polity Press, 2007.
Ignatiev, Noel, and John Garvey, ed. *Race Traitor.* New York: Routledge, 1996.
Ingram, David. *Habermas and the Dialectic of Reason.* New Haven: Yale University Press, 1987.
———. *Critical Theory and Philosophy.* New York: Paragon House, 1990.
———. *Group Rights: Reconciling Equality and Difference.* Lawrence, KS: University Press of Kansas, 2000.
———. *Rights, Democracy, and Fulfillment in the Era of Identity Politics: Principled Compromises in a Compromised World.* Lanham, MD: Rowman Littlefield, 2004.
———. "Toward a Cleaner White(ness): New Racial Identities," *Philosophical Forum* 36, no. 3 (2005): 243-77.
Kant, Immanuel. *Grounding for the Metaphysics of Morals,* 3rd ed. translated by James W. Ellington. Indianapolis: Hackett Publishing, 1993.
———. *Practical Philosophy.* translated by Mary Gregor. Cambridge: Cambridge University Press, 1996.
Kristeva, Julia. *Nations without Nationalism.* translated by Leon Roudiez. New York: Columbia University Press, 1993.
Kymlicka, Will, ed. *The Rights of Minority Cultures.* Oxford: Oxford University Press, 1995.
———. *Multicultural Citizenship: A Liberal Theory of Minority Rights.* Oxford: Oxford University Press, 1995.
———. "Do We Need a Liberal Theory of Minority Rights? Reply to Carens, Young, Parekh and Forst." *Constellations,* 4, no. 1 (1997): 72-87.
———. *Politics in the Vernacular: Nationalism, Multiculturalism, and Citizenship.* Oxford: Oxford University Press, 2002.
Macintyre, Alistair. *Whose Justice? Which Rationality?* South Bend, IN: University of Notre Dame Press, 1988.
Marcuse, Herbert. *One Dimensional Man.* Boston: Beacon Press, 1991.
Marx, Karl. "On the Jewish Question," in *Collected Works* vol. 3. New York: International Publishers, 1975: 146-74.
Mills, Charles. *The Racial Contract.* Ithaca: Cornell University Press, 1997.
———. *Blackness Visible: Essays on Philosophy and Race.* Ithaca: Cornell University Press, 1998.
Mouffe, Chantal. *The Democratic Paradox.* London: Verso, 2000.
Nussbaum, Martha. *Women and Human Development: The Capabilities Approach.* Cambridge: Cambridge University Press, 2000.
Outlaw, Lucius. *On Race and Philosophy.* New York: Routledge, 1996.
Rawls, John. "Reply to Habermas." In *Political Liberalism.* New York: Columbia University Press, 1996: 372-435.
———. *The Law of Peoples.* Cambridge, MA: Harvard University Press, 1999.
———. *Justice as Fairness: A Restatement.* Cambridge, MA: Harvard University Press, 2001.
Resnick, Judith. "Dependent Sovereign: Indian Tribes, States, and the Federal Courts," *University of Chicago Law Review* 56 (1989): 675-86.
Rousseau, Jean-Jacques. *Basic Political Writings.* Indianapolis, IN: Hackett Publishing, 1987.
Sandel, Michael. *Liberalism and the Limits of Justice.* Cambridge: Cambridge University Press, 1998.
Scheuerman, William. "Between Radicalism and Resignation: Democratic Theory in Habermas' *Between Facts and Norms*," in *Habermas: A Critical Reader.* Edited by Peter Dews. Oxford: Blackwell Publishers, 1999: 153-77.
Schmitt, Carl. *The Concept of the Political.* translated by George Schwab. Chicago: University of Chicago Press, 1996.
Sheehy, Paul. *The Reality of Social Groups.* Burlington: Ashgate Publishing, 2006.
Shelby, Tommie. *We Who Are Dark: The Philosophical Foundations of Black Solidarity.* Cambridge: Harvard University Press, 2005.

Taylor, Charles. *Sources of the Self: The Making of Modern Identity.* Cambridge: Cambridge University Press, 1989.

———. *Multiculturalism: Examining the Politics of Recognition.* Edited by Amy Gutmann. Princeton, NJ: Princeton University Press, 1994.

———. *Modern Social Imaginaries.* Durham, NC: Duke University Press, 2004.

Taylor, Paul. "Appiah's Uncompleted Argument: Du Bois and the Reality of Race," in *Social Theory and Practice* 26, no. 1 (2000): 103-28.

Walzer, Michael. *Spheres of Justice.* Oxford: Blackwell, 1983.

———. "On Involuntary Association," in *Freedom of Association.* Edited by Amy Gutmann. Princeton, NJ: Princeton University Press, 1998: 64-74.

Wilson, William Julius. *Social Justice in a Diverse Society.* Mountain View, CA: Mayfield, 1996.

Winant, Howard. *Racial Conditions.* Minneapolis: University of Minnesota Press, 1994.

Young, Iris M. *Justice and the Politics of Difference.* Princeton, NJ: Princeton University Press, 1990.

———. "Polity and Group Difference: A Critique of the Ideal of Group Citizenship," *Ethics*, 99, no. 2 (1989): 250-74.

Zack, Naomi. *Race and Mixed Race.* Philadelphia: Temple University Press, 1993.

———. *Philosophy of Science and Race.* New York: Routledge, 2002.

Index

Alcoff, Linda, 56, 70, 89, 111
Appiah, Kwame Anthony, 87, 103, 105–106
ascriptive identity, 2, 50

Bernier, Francois, 100
black identity, 120, 121
black nationalism, 119, 120–121

capability theory of rights, 61
Civil Rights Movement, 73, 89
class, 71, 91
collective identity, 4, 74. *See also* cultural identity; ethical-cultural identity; ethical-political identity; gender identity; Hispanic identity; racial identity
"color blind" social policy, 105
Combahee River Collective, 72, 77
constitutional patriotism., 82. *See also* ethical-political identity
constructivism, 74, 102
Cudd, Ann, 26
cultural identity, 49, 118
culture, 12, 13, 117–121
culture industry, 51

democracy, 80
democratic selection, 85–86
diaspora, 118
discourse ethic, 43, 82–83

distributive justice, 91
Doppelt, Gerald, 17
Du Bois, W.E.B, 102–104

eliminativism, 103, 105
ethical-cultural identity, 46
ethical-political identity, 46

feminism, 47, 73
Fraser, Nancy, 47, 52, 88
Frye, Marilyn, 25

gender identity, 74
Gould, Carol, 30–31
group rights, 58
Guiner, Lani and Gerald Torres, 78
Gutmann, Amy, 81

Habermas, Jurgen: on collective identity, 73; on multiculturalism, 58, 86; on the discourse ethic, 82–83; on oppression, 57; on rights, 40–41, 42, 58; Theory of Communicative Action, 52, 85; on structural transformation, 66n56, 71
Harlem Renaissance, 117
Haslanger, Sally, 28
hate crime, 24
Herr, Ranjoo Seodu, 12, 85
Hispanic identity, 23
Honneth, Axel, 59–60, 89

ideal theory, 34, 79, 96n26, 99
identity politics, 1, 5–6, 48, 63, 77, 81; criticisms of, 76, 89; and democracy, 80
Ignatiev, Noel, 114
immigration, 21
Ingram, David, 80, 87, 108, 113, 115
instrumental rationality, 53
intentionalism, 24, 74
intersubjectivity, 3–4, 60, 76

Kant, Immanuel, 42–43, 100–101
Kymlicka, Will, 2, 12–14, 16, 18

liberalism, 1, 19
lifeworld, 52, 114; colonization of, 53, 55. See also Habermas
Locke, Alain, 117

Marx, Karl, 19, 70, 91
mestizo identity, 111
Mills, Charles, 20–21, 54, 66n53, 66n54
mixed race, 110. See also mestizo identity
multicultural liberalism, 2, 11, 84

Native Americans, 22
Nussbaum, Martha, 61

oppression, 19, 25–29, 88
Outlaw, Lucius, 104, 107–108

personal identity, 74
proceduralism, 59

race, 100–105, 106–107. See also racial identity

racial identity, 7, 78, 105–106, 110–112. See also Hispanic identity; mestizo identity; white identity
Rawls, John, 80
recognition, 60
rights: moral vs. legal, 62; to self-ascription, 3, 4, 31, 59, 63. See also group rights
Rousseau, Jean-Jacques, 55

Santa Clara Pueblo v. Martinez, 83–84
Schmitt, Carl, 73
self-ascription. See rights
separatism, 109
Sheehy, Paul, 23, 37n67
Shelby, Tommie, 120–121
the social contract, 1, 76
symmetry thesis, 113

Taylor, Charles, 14–16
Taylor, Paul, 103
Theory of Communicative Action. See Habermas
Torres, Gerald and Lani Guinier, 78

Walzer, Michael, 33
Weber, Max, 51
white identity, 78, 112–116
Winant, Howard, 115
Wisconsin v. Mitchell, 36n41

Young, Iris Marion, 13, 29

Zack, Naomi, 110, 113